Who Murdered Lizzie?

Who Murdered Lizzie?

My Family Story of the Brutal Crime of 1884 that Shocked the City of Roanoke, Virginia

By Denise B. Tanaka

Published by Sasoriza Books

Published by Sasoriza Books
www.sasorizabooks.com
https://www.facebook.com/SasorizaBooks

Cover art by Fiona Jayde Media
https://fionajaydemedia.com

This one's for Dad

Table of Contents

Prologue

My father once told me, "One of my mother's sisters was murdered, possibly raped and strangled," when I started researching the family tree in the 1980s. Unfortunately, he could not recall details of an incident that had occurred decades before his birth. He could not say which of his aunts was the victim, or when, or even where the murder occurred.

Researching this cold case meant overcoming a number of challenges. First is the lack of accurate information about our family history. My late father enjoyed spinning yarns over the supper table, such as claiming a relation to President Woodrow Wilson for whom he was named. Yet he had no hard evidence for any of his colorful anecdotes, no letters or documents, no family bible, and only a handful of un-labeled sepia photographs.

When I first started researching my grandmother's family line, all I had was her maiden name Isabelle Marie Wilson. My father only knew that her family came from

England, and she was born in Ohio in 1880. Grandmother died when my father was 10 years old. He lost touch with his cousins, aunts, and uncles as the years passed and he moved to California.

Also, the timelines in my family are unusually long and spread out. When I first heard this story, I did not know that 100 years had passed since the crime. Both pairs of my grandparents were married in the early 20th century. Within a couple of generations, I am transported to the era of Charles Dickens, the antebellum South, and the beginnings of the Industrial Revolution. My grandparents were among the youngest of many siblings. My parents were in their forties when I was born the last child in our family. My father was next-to-youngest of six siblings. When I began the work of identifying monochrome faces in fading photographs, many of the aunts, uncles, and older cousins had long since died. Keepsakes and family mementos had been lost to the years.

Another challenge is that my grandmother's parents had the frustratingly common names of John and Elizabeth Wilson. They never owned real estate or stayed in one place for very long. As a working-class family struggling to find better jobs, they relocated every few years. I have spent decades (before the internet) searching for Wilson needles in a global haystack, painstakingly reconstructing a brick mason's vagabond life.

Piece by piece, I collected census records and birth certificates. My grandmother's birth and death certificates confirmed her parents' names. The U.S. federal census of 1880 in Ohio listed my grandmother's older siblings: five born in England, and two born in Canada. Lucky for me, one of the Canadian birth records was a "delayed registration" actually completed in 1925 and signed by an older sister living in Roanoke, Virginia who attested to being present at the birth. Following this clue, I found proof of my Wilson family in the 1900 census of Virginia.

From time to time, I tried to find records of a teenaged girl's murder. I wrote to librarians in Ohio and Virginia, but without a date or even the name of which child was killed, they turned up nothing.

I corresponded with third-generation cousins who knew even less than I did. My cousins who joined the Daughters of the American Revolution had narrowed the focus of their research to the maternal lines of spouses who married my grandmother's siblings. They had no interest in wading through a quagmire of Wilson brick masons in England. So the trail went cold.

For decades, that elusive mystery kept nagging at me. I moved on with my life, working full-time and supporting my own family. On the weekends, I dabbled in genealogy to fill out my family tree. I kept thinking of someone in our family whose tragic death had been forgotten by the next generation. Which of my great aunts was murdered? When? Where? How?

One summer, a lucky search on Google Books turned up a clue. Ironically, I was only collecting local history books with general information about the city of Roanoke, Virginia. I looked within the text for "brick" to learn more about brick makers and stone masons in the area. I was hoping to get a picture of John Wilson's working class life in the developing boom town. By chance, the search hit popped up with Rand Dotson's history of Roanoke, Virginia published in 2007.

> Lizzie Wilson, age 14, was attacked while walking home one evening, possibly raped, and brutally murdered with her throat cut from ear to ear. The authorities never solved the mystery.

I latched onto that clue and dug deeper. I learned the exact date of the crime was November 4, 1884, the night of the presidential election. Her name "Lizzie" and her age matched what I knew from the census of 1880 that the Wilsons had a daughter Elizabeth born in 1870. The time frame fit because the family had moved from Ohio to Roanoke, Virginia before 1889 when their youngest son Walter was born. Dotson's book summarized old newspaper accounts of the family's working class origins and the fact that the Wilsons had just moved to Roanoke hoping to better their life in the developing city. With little else to go on, my guts told me... *This is her.*

Now, with a name and a date, my search of historic newspapers uncovered a treasure trove of sensational articles. My father's aunt was like the JonBenét Ramsey of the 1880s in making national headlines. The local community rallied around the Wilson family. The city council offered a cash reward and hired out-of-town detectives to work the case.

Here for the first time is the whole story of what happened when my great-aunt Lizzie Wilson was murdered.

The Murder

At the time of her murder on the night of November 4, 1884, Elizabeth Jane "Lizzie" Wilson had recently turned 14 years old. She attended public school in the growing boom town of Roanoke, Virginia. She also worked an afternoon job at a bakery to help support her large family.

Lizzie felt no fear of being a stranger on unfamiliar city streets; she had been the new girl in town several times in her short life. The Wilson family had just arrived in Roanoke, Virginia the year before. Always in search of better opportunities and greener grass on the other side of the hill, this family had led a vagabond existence. Roanoke felt like one more stop on the adventurous trail of her life thus far.

That fateful Tuesday evening was also Election Day for the nation. Everyone's nerves were on edge from coast to coast. Anticipation of national change filled the air. The poet Walt Whitman described the power of voting in his poem *Election Day November 1884* as "The stretch of

North and South arous'd — sea-board and inland — Texas to Maine — the Prairie States — Vermont, Virginia, California, the final ballot-shower from East to West — the paradox and conflict, the countless snow-flakes falling — a swordless conflict... the peaceful choice of all..."

Democratic candidate Grover Cleveland of New York ran against Republican candidate James G. Blaine of Maine. A majority of Americans did not strongly favor either of these two men. Contemporary newspapers sizzled with sensational mudslinging and scandals. Cleveland was accused of fathering an illegitimate child, and Blaine was exposed for high-level financial corruption. In the following days, the winner would be announced by razor-thin margins. In an eerie parallel to our presidential elections in recent years, the electoral map of 1884 shows a United States divided sharply in half by large patches of red and blue. Grover Cleveland won the popular vote by 48.9% and 219 electoral votes, carrying the South and several key swing states. James Blaine came in a close second with a popular vote of 48.3% and 182 electoral votes.

A handful of third-party candidates tried to shake up the status quo but only took a small percentage of the national popular vote. Most notably, a lawyer named

Belva Ann Lockwood was the first woman to run a national campaign as a strategic push for women's suffrage. (Women would not gain the right to vote in national elections for another 35 years with ratification of the 19th Amendment to the U.S. Constitution.) "I cannot vote but I can be voted for," she said in one of her campaign speeches. In the end, Lockwood received over 4,000 votes nationally.

Roanoke's male citizens gathered on the evening of this Election Day in a warehouse to listen for news of the results by wire. A well-established network of telegraph lines could quickly transmit news from coast to coast, which meant rapid reporting of ballots being counted from New York to California. They must have expected the biggest news in the coming days to be whether a Democrat or a Republican took the presidency. Twenty years after the end of the Civil War, and with the dawn of the Industrial Revolution, they must have felt that the country was on the verge of a new modern era.

Those who did not care about politics gathered in saloons to drink away their Tuesday evening. Others simply went about their daily business, laboring in the railroad's machine shops or bringing home supper for their families.

Somewhere among all of these men outside of their homes that night, there lurked a murderer.

===

Lizzie Wilson worked her usual afternoon shift at a bakery-confectionary shop owned by Mr. Harry Toole. The exact location of the shop is unclear but several accounts place it either on Salem Avenue or its parallel street Norfolk Avenue in the southwest quadrant of the city. Lizzie's route to her home on Madison Avenue, in the northeast, was a nearly straight line at a 45 degree angle. However, she would need to cross the sprawling railroad tracks and navigate around newly-constructed brick buildings on half-developed city streets.

Roanoke's downtown was still a work in progress. Unpaved roads of weeds and mud reeked of poor sanitation: human, horse, and livestock waste. A few gas-lit streetlamps offered faint glimmering spots against the darkness. Many streets had no lights at all. After sunset, Lizzie relied on the glow of the full moon to light her way home.

It was not safe for a young woman to walk the streets alone after dark. As with any large city, violent crime was not contained entirely to any one part of town. The city had its patches of notoriously rough neighborhoods, such as "Brick Row" to the southeast. Around the railroad yards, drunken men in the saloons assaulted each other daily. Roanoke's lone sheriff could hardly contain the mayhem.

Lizzie's older sister Caroline Alice Wilson, who was 18 years old on that night, came to the bakery to accompany her home. The newspapers do not mention if Alice had a job as well, perhaps in the farmer's market square near the railway station, but it makes sense. Their father was a brick mason by trade and hardly a wealthy man of leisure. All of the children had worked from an early age.

The sisters had done this routine many times before and felt safer walking together. Hand-in-hand, the young women projected an air of confidence as they walked swiftly the route they knew so well. Passers-by on the streets may have assumed the girls to be older than their true age, as the Wilson family trait is to be slender and tall.

Someone could have stalked Lizzie from the bakery's door, or someone could have encountered her at random along the way home.

Alice and Lizzie crossed the multiple lines of railroad tracks after carefully looking both ways. They passed through the shadow of the city's landmark Hotel Roanoke that their father a brick mason had a hand in constructing. The girls walked northward up Commonwealth Avenue NE on their way to Madison Avenue. From door to door, the distance was about one mile. It would have taken under 30 minutes to make the trip.

Their mother may have been in the kitchen preparing supper or hanging the day's laundry. Her husband's work shirts and the soiled clothing of eight children surely kept her busy at the washboard. While waiting for Alice and Lizzie to walk home, Mrs. Wilson had four more daughters under the age of 12: Annie, Georgiana, my grandmother Isabelle Marie, and little Sadie a two-year-old toddler. Another son, Albert, was almost seven years old.

Their older brother William, age 16, was reading a book in the warmth of the kitchen. Like his sisters, he probably worked a part-time menial job while attending school. He would have a few hours by lamplight to do his homework. On this cool Tuesday evening, he propped his stockinged feet on the pot-belly iron stove.

Lizzie became impatient to get home. By now, they were so close! It was about 7:00 or 8:00 o'clock and getting colder by the minute. Despite the full moon, the streets were pitch dark. Somewhere between the cross-streets of Gilmer and Rutherford Avenue, Lizzie broke away from her sister. Challenging Alice with laughter, Lizzie made a fatal mistake by taking a short cut across an undeveloped field.

Alice did not have the courage to follow her sister into the tall grass and dandelions. Perhaps she called out to her, "Lizzie, no, let's stay together!" For the rest of her life, Alice would second-guess her decision to let Lizzie go alone. Instead, she chose to run a safer route by staying on the dimly-lit, muddy streets.

Despite taking the longer route, Alice won the race. She had nearly reached the front porch of their home when she looked back.

Lizzie emerged from the vacant field. She set one foot on the boards of the street's sidewalk. She smiled one last time, within plain view of her home, her family, and safety.

Two men grabbed Lizzie. They dragged her backwards into the darkness. She shrieked and they

7

muffled her mouth. Within seconds, they vanished into the bushes of the empty field.

Alice screamed for help. Crying in panic, she dashed up the front doorsteps.

William jumped to his feet, dropped his book, and grabbed a gun. He dashed outside wearing only his socks. Pointing the barrel of his gun into the darkness, he saw no signs of movement. Lizzie and her attackers had vanished in the night.

Lizzie's mother rushed into the street. The younger children came as far as the front porch to stare wide-eyed at the chaotic scene. Clutching her apron, Mrs. Wilson screamed frantically at her neighbors' homes. The housing complex was a cluster of closely-packed windows and doors. Before long, dozens of fellow railroad workers dashed outside to help.

Men and teenaged boys rushed into the streets to answer the alarm. By the light of a waning full moon, they searched the alleyways and surrounding vacant fields. Carrying lanterns and rifles, they called Lizzie's name into the darkness.

John Wilson, her father, is not mentioned in any of the newspaper reports. It is unclear if he was home at the time of the attack. Perhaps he worked late at a construction site, or he made a habit of loitering with friends after a long day's work. He may have stood among the crowds gathered to listen for the clickety-click of the telegraph announcing results of the presidential election. If he had applied for citizenship while the family lived in Ohio, he could have voted in this election for a U.S. president for the first time in his life. He might have been socializing with his fellow bricklayers at the Masonic Lodge when his daughter was murdered.

Search parties found her body roughly 100 yards from where she had been snatched. Lizzie's attackers, fearing capture, had slashed her throat with a razor. They dumped her in the grass and fled the scene. She bled out where she lay face-down in a pile of tattered clothes.

Lizzie's Route Home

Starting from Mr. Toole's bakery in the southwest part of town, Lizzie and her sister walked northeast up Commonwealth Avenue on their way home to Madison Avenue NE.

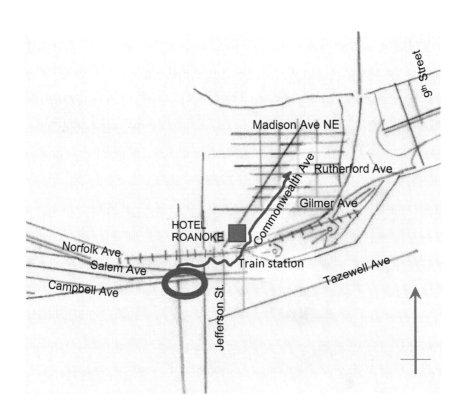

This illustration is based on several historical maps. Since 1884, renovations and developments have significantly changed downtown Roanoke. Many streets no longer exist. Today, the highway Route 220 runs through town.

The Manhunt

All of that long night and into Wednesday, the neighbors searched for clues to identify Lizzie's attackers. As Wednesday rolled into Thursday, the hours dragged on while the murderers remained at large. Word of this gruesome crime spread quickly. Men organized into vigilante groups to patrol the streets. Women and children were in constant terror, sheltering behind locked doors and feeling afraid to go outside after nightfall. The terrifying aspect of the random brutality shook everyone to their core. Although the rough-and-tumble sections of town had their share of alcohol-driven saloon fights and stabbings, this crime felt different.

The local city newspaper, *The Roanoke Leader*, printed the breaking news on Thursday, November 6, 1884. Their haste to go to press sacrificed the accuracy of some details such as Lizzie's exact age or whether it was a younger sister who witnessed her being snatched.

> MURDER — One of the foulest murders ever perpetrated occurred in this city about 7 o'clock on the evening of November 4th. A

young girl about 15 or 16 years of age, by name, Lizzie Wilson, was seized on the sidewalk at the corner of Rutherford Street and Commonwealth Avenue, by two men who carried her by force about 100 yards away on the common, where her throat was cut and she was held by the brutes until she bled to death. When she was seized, she screamed and her little sister, who was only about 50 yards away, saw two men have hold of Lizzie and ran and told her mother, who at once alarmed the neighborhood and many started in search of the girl and soon found her dead body. The citizens soon became aware of the murder, and hundreds visited the place, and search parties started in all directions to try and trace the murderers. Had they been found, in all probability they would have been lynched immediately under the excitement of the moment.

Newspapers broadcast the story on the wire, spreading within hours from Virginia to Maryland and as far north as the *New York Times*. Headlines such as "Victim of a Foul Wretch," and "A Young Lady's Throat Cut," competed with the announcement of President Grover Cleveland's election. The essential facts were embellished with graphic descriptions of the young girl's injuries, her throat cut "ear to ear" and her clothing in tatters to suggest that a sexual assault had also happened. In those days before television or radio news broadcasts, people read newspapers aloud to each other in small groups. One can imagine an excited narrator with a large sheet of paper clutched in hand and a circle of horrified, awestruck listeners.

===

Meanwhile, as the citizens of Roanoke were in an uproar, the Wilsons had the sad task of making arrangements to bury a child. Their grief and trauma are beyond comprehension. Although the crime happened over 100 years ago, the tragedy of parents losing a child to a random act of violence is timeless. The hard-working bricklayer and his wife were thrust into unwanted celebrity status. Hundreds of strangers from the neighborhood or from the churches surrounded them with outpourings of sympathy. I imagine the Wilsons felt grateful but also overwhelmed with the burden of so much attention.

From our modern perspective of television news and social media, it seems strange that I cannot find any newspaper articles that include personal interviews with the Wilson family. Clearly, a different style of journalism existed in those days. Reporters avoided harassing the parents and siblings of the murdered girl. The Wilsons are mentioned from a distance but they are not on public

13

display; their heartbreak was not exploited to sell more newspapers.

The "Register of City of Roanoke Deaths for 1884" is a handwritten ledger book of names, preserved at the Virginia Room of the Roanoke Library. Her tragic death is recorded with clinical brevity in a simple line entry:

> (*Name*) Wilson, Elizabeth J.; (*Race*) White; (*Sex*) F.; (*Date of Death*) Nov. 4; (*Place of Death*) Roanoke City; (*Name of Disease or Cause of Death*) Murdered; (*Age*) 14; (*Names of Parents*) John and E.J. Wilson.

Reverend William C. Campbell, pastor of the First Presbyterian Church, counseled and comforted the Wilson family in their time of need. They held the funeral at his church and, no doubt, hundreds of townsfolk attended. The city council donated the cost of a burial plot in the City Cemetery and paid for a lovely white marble tombstone. Years later, as part of his reminiscences on Roanoke's past tragedies, Reverend Campbell wrote a personal account of the incident. "It was in the early evening and at the corner of a much-frequented street. I have never seen a community so terrorized as Roanoke

14

was by this murder. It was so bold and brutal and mysterious that people were afraid to leave their homes after dark." Since Reverend Campbell's arrival in Roanoke in 1881, he had witnessed and condemned the alarming rise in lawlessness — drunkenness, gambling, prostitution, gunfights, stabbings, and midnight prowlers. In Lizzie's senseless murder, all of his worst fears had come to pass.

===

Within days of Lizzie's funeral, a number of affluent businessmen called a Citizens' Meeting. They gathered in Rorer Hall at 3rd Street and Campbell Avenue. They formed a committee to collect funds to be spent in the pursuit of justice. The group included: Henry S. Trout, president of the First National Bank of Roanoke and son of Big Lick's former mayor; Peyton Leftwich Terry, a merchant and former member of Big Lick's town council who was also Henry Trout's brother-in-law; Charles Lunsford, elected as chairman of the citizens' committee, who owned the first and largest insurance underwriting businesses in town; and, Dr. Joseph A. Gale, a physician and surgeon employed by the railroad.

Henry Trout proposed for the committee to appropriate $500 to supplement the reward offered by the

City Council for the apprehension of the murderer. This resolution passed by unanimous vote and would be announced in the newspapers as a total $1,000 reward. That was an extraordinary amount of money in 1884, equivalent to over $28,000 today.

Reverend Lewis L. Lloyd offered a resolution condemning mob law, urging all good citizens to aid in its suppression, which the committee passed unanimously. As businessmen and real estate investors, they may have been concerned for their growing city's public reputation as a lawless Wild West town. After all, Wyatt Earp's legendary gunfight at the O.K. Corral in Tombstone, Arizona had occurred just three years before.

On the following day, *The Roanoke Leader* printed an anonymous editorial that admonished the city's residents from devolving into a raging lynch mob.

> "That the foul murder committed in this city on Tuesday evening should have excited widespread indignation in the community is not surprising, and we have the fullest assurance that the authorities will spare no effort to bring the author or authors of this crime to justice. Meantime we hear of threats of lynching one of the parties already arrested. It is as well to understand now, as when it is too late, that such a course will not be tolerated. The Mayor has

authority in such cases to call out the military and firemen if need be to protect a prisoner, and will assuredly do so if an attempt of the kind in question is made. Lynch law, under the strongest provocation, and with unquestioned evidence of the guilt of the prisoner, is always to be reprobated; how much more, therefore, is it to be condemned in the case of an arrested party against whom only a vague suspicion rests magnified a thousand-fold by idle gossip, as in the present instance. We sincerely hope that in the interest of justice, as well as for the good name of the city, our people will keep cool and the wiser control the restless spirits that may be indisposed to allow the law to take its course with all parties who may be arrested."

===

The scene of the crime, the city of Roanoke, was hardly a well-established urban center like London or New York. Lizzie's murder happened while the city was experiencing its Industrial Revolution growing pains and transformation into an urban hub. Until the early 1880s, this quiet farming town in southwestern Virginia was called Big Lick. Fields of tobacco and wheat thrived in the fertile lands. Livestock grazed on the green hillsides. Plentiful springs and the Roanoke River provided clear water. The river also provided power for the grist mills that turned wheat or corn into flour. When the Virginia &

17

Tennessee Railroad company built the first line of tracks in the 1850s, Big Lick and the nearby town of Salem held a central position for the transportation of goods (especially tobacco) produced in region.

During the American Civil War (from 1861 to 1865), the young men of Roanoke County volunteered for Confederate service and deployed to battlefields farther to the east and south. This region of the Shenandoah Valley, close to the border of Tennessee, was too far inland to be of much strategic importance and experienced less damage than eastern coastal states like Georgia. The northern troops ventured into southwestern Virginia on just two occasions. The first time, they burned the train depot, destroyed several miles of tracks, and seized supplies from a warehouse. The second time, Union forces engaged in a skirmish with Confederate troops but that incident did not quite rise to the level of a major battle.

When the Civil War ended with the South's surrender, the defeated soldiers returned home. Changes occurred in the political landscape—slavery was abolished—but in many ways the cultural landscape of the valley remained the same. The wealthier citizens, the former slave owners and Confederate officers did not easily relinquish their dominance. They passed through the decades of Reconstruction and economic recovery to emerge relatively unscathed. They changed their gray uniforms for business suits. By retaining ownership of large tracts of land, by converting their plantations into profitable real estate, many of them preserved their position on top of the social pyramid.

In the early 1880s, the neighboring towns of Big Lick and Salem competed with each other to negotiate a deal with the railroads. The Norfolk & Western Railway company wanted to build a new depot, hotels, and mercantile shops. Prosperity would be guaranteed for whichever town the railroad selected to become a major railroad hub for the Shenandoah Valley. A group of affluent local citizens negotiated a deal, raised the necessary investment capital, and convinced the railroad to choose Big Lick over Salem.

Before the coming of the railroad, the population of Big Lick was about seven hundred. Within two or three years, the population exploded to over five thousand. Big Lick transformed overnight into the so-called "Magic City" of Roanoke. Agriculture gave way to industrialization. Factories sprang out of the marshlands. Newcomers flooded into town from all directions, hoping to find a better life after several years of a nationwide economic recession. Strangers filled the streets with the traffic of unfamiliar faces; no longer did passers-by recognize their fellow church-goers, cousins, and in-laws. Migrants occupied hastily-erected housing projects that sprouted in the downtown.

===

Lizzie's father John Satchell Wilson was a lifelong bricklayer and mason like his father before him. John Wilson brought his family out of England in the mid-1870s when Lizzie was a small child. They never stayed in one place for long, following one construction project after another. Since their arrival in North America, the family relocated three times in 10 years: from Stratford, Ontario to Cleveland, Ohio and finally to Roanoke, Virginia.

Lizzie's mother perpetually had toddlers clinging to her skirts whenever she packed up the household belongings to follow her husband to the next opportunity. Mrs. Wilson held the family together across the Atlantic Ocean, across the Great Lakes, and over the Appalachian Mountains only to find tragedy at the end of the rainbow.

Bricklayers like Lizzie Wilson's father were needed to construct the factory buildings, the shops, the banks, the landmarks such as the Hotel Roanoke and Hotel Ponce de Leon, and the multi-story office buildings for the railroad's executive headquarters. John Wilson heard the call and convinced his wife, once more, to uproot their family from Cleveland, Ohio. He may have enticed her with promises of greener pastures, blue skies, and fresh air. The Blue Ridge and Allegheny mountains sheltered the valley from harsh weather. For the Wilsons coming from England, from Canada, and from northern Ohio, the mild winters of rural Virginia must have appeared as a very attractive prospect.

Upon arriving in Roanoke City, the Wilson family rented a room in the housing complex known as Brick Row in the southeast section of the city. They are listed in a local census taken by the town council in December 1883. They joined the ranks of over a thousand newcomers who came as labor for the manufacturing industries. Local tobacco processing factories shut down to make room for the railroad's offices and machine works. Within a few short years, Roanoke became a manufacturing center for world-class steam locomotives and freight cars. As a bricklayer, John Wilson and his fellow masons constructed many of the new buildings for the "Magic City" of Roanoke. Their names carry no prestige in the local history books, yet the elegant hotels and high-rise municipal buildings would not exist without their handiwork.

In the following year after their arrival, the Wilsons had saved enough money to rent a home from the Roanoke Land & Improvement Company in the northeast area of the city. They left behind the rough Brick Row neighborhood where the abundant saloons and brothels had devolved into a dangerous place with epidemic drunkenness and violent muggings.

By moving to the northeast part of town, to company housing on Madison Avenue N.E., the Wilsons must have thought that their lives were improving day by day. Their optimism was forever shattered by the senseless murder of their young daughter.

The Accused

A number of suspects were arrested immediately but released for lack of evidence. In the days and weeks that followed November 4, 1884, vigilante groups became more desperate. Self-appointed posses seized upon anyone who appeared vaguely suspicious. Police exonerated every man dragged to the jailhouse, including a fellow described only as "an itinerant ink peddler" by the *Richmond Dispatch*. The citizens' committee published a notice in *The Roanoke Leader* that chastised the vigilantes for another such case of hasty arrest, noting that the man's "reputation has been sullied, his business injured and a great wrong done him."

Frenzied, frivolous accusations spread to the surrounding towns. For example, on November 8, 1884, the *Alexandria Gazette* reported: "A suspicious character named Ross, who claimed to be from Suffolk, was arrested in Christiansburg yesterday by a depot agent and sent to Roanoke, charged with the murder of Lizzie Wilson. His shirt sleeves were covered with blood."

One has to wonder if Lizzie's older sister Alice — the only eyewitness — was called to the sheriff's office on multiple occasions. Would they have asked her to try and make an identification each time they had a new suspect behind bars? Considering the late hour and dark of night, even the perpetrators' race could not possibly be determined. Most of the vigilante groups assumed with utter certainty that the murderers were two African-American men. In reality, they could have been dark-complexioned white men or outdoor laborers with dirty faces. The investigators at the sheriff's office kept a more open mind; no one was above suspicion.

Harry Toole, the owner of the bakery-confectionary store where Lizzie had worked, was also considered a person of interest. Sheriff Webber questioned Mr. Toole but, for lack evidence, did not make an arrest. Shortly thereafter, Mr. Toole fled town, abandoning his wife and two small children. He vanished for parts unknown only to resurface six years later in Anniston, Alabama. Mr. Toole took a second wife and fathered at least one more child. A local Alabama newspaper called him the proprietor of one of Anniston's most notorious "blind tigers," that is, an establishment illegally selling liquor. Long before the infamous 18th

Amendment to the U.S. Constitution that prohibited the production, transport, and sale of alcohol, a number of states had passed local laws to prohibit alcohol sales within their jurisdiction.

Illegally selling liquor in Alabama was not Harry Toole's only offense. Since he had not divorced his first wife, Toole was charged with bigamy. Roanoke's chief of police travelled to Alabama to answer a court summons in Toole's case and to pursue the fugitive. The *Richmond Dispatch* newspaper, June 29, 1890, reported on Mr. Toole's situation. "This recalls a sad case in the annals of Roanoke. Six years ago, Lizzie Wilson, a pretty girl of fourteen years, was foully murdered in the eastern part of the city." The short article concludes with this: "A trace of him has been kept by the police and he will no doubt be run down and placed behind the bars, charged with the outrageous act."

Nevertheless, Harry Toole was not arrested for Lizzie Wilson's murder. He vanished into obscurity after abandoning his two wives and a handful of children. Could this shadowy character be a prime suspect? Perhaps he had a violent urge to dominate the innocent teenaged girl who worked under him. Alternatively, the owner of this so-called confectionary shop may have conducted illegal activities out of the back room. Perhaps Lizzie saw something she should not have seen. Perhaps some unsavory character stalked Lizzie on her walk home?

===

A dark Christmas passed and the New Year came for the grieving Wilson family. The youngest boy, Albert, turned seven years old in January 1885 but I cannot imagine there was much joy to be had at the celebration.

The hardest birthday must have been for William who turned 17 years old in March 1885. For several months, teenaged William carried the burden of grief and rage while waiting for news of his sister's murderers to be found. I wonder if William participated in the search parties or the citizens' patrols or if he carried a gun in the streets to protect his surviving sisters.

The Roanoke City Council hired three investigators from the world-renowned Pinkerton Detective Agency to assist the local sheriff. The FBI would not exist until 1908, and so, with limited resources, the city was running out of options for finding the murderer.

===

In the spring of 1885, two men were accused of the crime. The police had no evidence against them, no clear identification from the eyewitness, and a flimsy excuse for an arrest. Nonetheless, after six months of a fruitless manhunt, Roanoke's sheriff felt overwhelming pressure to close the case by putting someone — anyone — on trial.

Lewis Watkins and Wilson Steptoe, the accused, were hardly strangers in town. These lifelong friends and brothers-in-law were a pair of single, young Black men who had lived in or around Big Lick for their entire lives. Born enslaved, they became free citizens of the United States at an early age which set them apart from the experiences of their older siblings and their parents.

Watkins and Steptoe were the first generation of free young men struggling to find their place in a world where the Confederacy was defeated but not so easily swept away. I have discovered some facts about the family background of these two young men. However, I cannot presume to understand a fraction of what their lives were like beyond what is generally known about Roanoke's African-American community. It was another world, another time.

Their parents had lived their entire lives enslaved, only gaining their freedom in middle age. Both of their fathers, William Watkins and Caesar Steptoe, proudly registered to vote for the first time in the Reconstruction period after the end of the war. The *Poll Book of Colored Voters in the 4th District of Roanoke Co., Va.* (1867) from the Library of Virginia records the voters who participated in elections. Elections were held October 22, 1867, while Virginia was under federal military rule, and were the first elections in which African Americans were allowed to vote.

Yet their former masters did not simply vanish after the surrender at Appomattox. Confederate soldiers and officers returned home not to disgrace but to sympathy for their glorious "lost cause." They retained ownership of land and made a profit on real estate. They continued to carry their rank titles, such as Colonel, and former soldiers freely boasted of their wounds earned valiantly on the battlefield. They took seats on the town council, became judges, sheriffs, businessmen, and clergy. Their biographies were published in local history books, with honors, often lauding their daring deeds of military strategy.

The accomplishments of Roanoke's African-American citizens were wholly ignored in the annals of local histories. Deprived of a family heritage, their existence was noted in official records as items of household inventory. They created few records themselves. In addition, Southern states suffered the destruction of many official records during the war or natural disasters. Many states did not mandate recording births, marriages, or deaths until after 1900. Even African-Americans whose ancestors were free before 1865 may find challenges if their ancestors moved frequently, worked for others, and owned no land. As a researcher, I feel fortunate to have uncovered what little I have on the Watkins and Steptoe families.

===

Lewis Watkins was a middle child in between three elder and three younger siblings. His parents William and Sophie Watkins were not allowed to be legally married while enslaved, but they "commenced cohabitation" as husband and wife in September 1859. This information comes from the Library of Virginia's *Register of Colored Persons of Roanoke County, State of Virginia, Cohabiting Together as Husband and Wife on February 27, 1866*. A cohabitation register was the legal vehicle by which formerly enslaved people legitimized both their marriages and their children. The information about an individual person contained in a cohabitation register is literally priceless as it is often the first time that they were officially recognized in a public record.

His father William Watkins, a blacksmith, was born circa 1830 in Botetourt County, Virginia enslaved by a man named William Nofsinger. His wife Sophie Wright was born circa 1828 in Franklin County, Virginia. She was last owned by J.H. Smith—possibly the same John H. Smith in the 1870 federal census of Big Lick. Apparently, after the Civil War, the Watkins family continued to live and work on Smith's farm as laborers or sharecroppers.

The practice of sharecropping emerged when Southern landowners no longer had free labor to maintain their crops of tobacco or corn. Former masters offered jobs to the same people they had enslaved, to work the same farmlands not for wages but in exchange for a portion of the crop. These laborers earned anywhere from a quarter to a half of the harvest to feed themselves or to sell at the farmers' market. The problem was that formerly enslaved people had no capital to invest in farms of their own and were forced to buy necessities on credit. They often continued to live in their old homes alongside neighbors who were in the same boat. Often, the former masters swindled their workers out of the promised payoff. Any remaining debt was rolled into the next year with added interest. Workers were trapped, lacking the means to leave a farm until their debts were paid in full. By contrast, southern state governments granted pensions to Confederate veterans and their widows; even in losing the war, the former slave owners came out on top.

A decade later, the lives of the Watkins family changed somewhat for the better. In the 1880 federal census of Big Lick, the father William Watkins was the head of his own household. He worked as a blacksmith along with his son Price. I wonder if some of his customers for horseshoes and wagon wheels were the same men who had once enslaved him, his wife, and his children. Lewis Watkins, age 22 in the summer of 1880, had a job as a farm laborer.

===

Wilson Steptoe was also something of a middle child, with five older and two younger siblings. His parents "commenced cohabitation" as husband and wife in December 1846, according to the register. Cesar Steptoe was born circa 1820 in Bedford County enslaved by J.H. Smith — possibly the same John H. Smith who had owned Lewis Watkins's mother. His wife Laura was born circa 1825 in Botetourt County. Her last owner was G.W.

Carr — possibly the George W. Carr living on a nearby farm in the 1870 census.

The Steptoe families lived three doors away from the Watkins family in the 1880 federal census of Big Lick. In that year, Wilson Steptoe's parents Caesar and Laura had only two of their sons living at home. Other children had moved out to make homes and families of their own. The parents worked as farm laborers and both young men worked in the tobacco factory.

Lewis Watkins and Wilson Steptoe were not just lifelong friends but they also became brothers-in-law. Lewis's brother William Watkins married Wilson's sister Lavinia Steptoe in 1876; and, in the 1880 federal census Wilson's sister Lucy Steptoe lived in William's home to help care for the couple's three small children.

Next door was the home of Wilson's brother George Steptoe and his wife Ida Rossie who also worked in the tobacco factory. As of the 1880 federal census, they had a baby named Henry. They lived near the homes of their parents, all within calling distance of each other's front door.

===

The Watkins and Steptoe families lived in a unique time in American history, during the transition from centuries of slavery into the early years of citizenship. When the Civil War ended, it meant emancipation for about one-third of Roanoke County's population. For the first time, these formerly enslaved people could purchase real estate, own businesses, earn wages, get married and raise families of their own. Yet the communities were sharply divided along racial lines within the towns of Salem and Roanoke. They coalesced into close-knit neighborhoods restricted by the value of real estate, by who was willing to sell land to whom, or who was willing to buy a home near "colored" neighbors. Annual city directories (the precursor to phone books) marked its non-white citizens with an asterisk next to their names.

The segregated communities surrounding the city had picturesque names such as Big Hill, Twine Hollow, and Gum Spring. Within the city limits of Roanoke, the neighborhood on Tenth Avenue was known as Peach and Honey, and an area to the northeast beyond Madison Avenue was called Possum Trot. The largest group of Black residents lived in the town of Gainsborough, to the northwest, dubbed the Bunker Hill neighborhood after its absorption into Roanoke's city limits.

The majority of African-Americans worked as unskilled labor, but not all were factory workers, sharecroppers, or manual laborers. Gradually there would also be business owners and professionals who assumed leadership roles in the Black community. They came to own grocery stores, butcher shops, boarding houses, and barber shops. Not at first, but by the 1890s there would be lawyers, doctors, and teachers. A man named Andrew Jackson Oliver earned a law degree in Ohio and in 1890 opened Roanoke's first African-American law office. Dr. Robert J. Boland opened Roanoke's first Black medical practice in 1891. Dr. Boland also published the *Roanoke Weekly Press, Colored* — the town's only African-American newspaper.

Schools emerged, built with funding from the federal Freedmen's Bureau, missionary associations, and African Americans themselves. Mostly white, female teachers came with missionary groups to educate the newly-freed people who, in the antebellum South, had been prevented from learning to read or write. One notable exception was Lucy Addison, born enslaved in Fauquier County, Virginia. She graduated from the Institute for Colored Youth in Philadelphia and attended Howard University. Ms. Addison came to Roanoke in

1887 to teach at Gainsborough Elementary school. She would continue to work in education for the next 40 years, becoming principal of the Harrison School and expanding on the curriculum. Based upon her leadership contributions, Ms. Addison would be honored in 1928 with the naming of a new high school—the first such honor offered to any resident of the City of Roanoke.

===

The two accused men, Lewis Watkins and Wilson Steptoe, experienced very different lives from their parents and older siblings. Baseball games brought crowds together of all races and classes, although with class- and gender-specific spectator seating. Non-whites were relegated to standing beyond the outfield fence. The Roanoke Athletic Association organized the first official baseball game in May 1883 and the Roanoke players defeated a team from the nearby town of Salem. In the summer of 1883, the first African-American team "Roanoke Slippers" formed but they were prohibited from playing against white teams.

As these young men Lewis Watkins and Wilson Steptoe grew into their twenties, all they knew of the antebellum period came from stories told by their parents and older siblings. They had not experienced slavery first-hand but grew up in the aftermath with segregated communities and labor exploitation. Promises of freedom, change, and new opportunities — ringing in their ears for their entire lives — sounded hollower by the day.

After the rapid transformation of rural Big Lick into urban Roanoke in the 1880s, the tobacco factory shut down. Unemployment swept like a plague through the African-American men of the city. Jobs became harder to find in the volatile boom/slump economy of a city growing its industry faster than it could lay bricks on its muddy streets. The newly created jobs of mechanics, bricklayers, or railroad engineers were being taken by working-class white immigrants from the north. The influx of outsiders — Yankees and disgruntled Southerners both — came to "The Magic City" looking for a new life. Farmers of tobacco or corn struggled to compete with machinists and engineers. The old-timers in town felt overwhelmed and resentful as their opportunities for a better life evaporated before their eyes.

===

Lewis Watkins and Wilson Steptoe were accused of attempted rape by a white woman identified by name only as "Mays" in the *Staunton Spectator*, April 29, 1885. Miss Mays alleged that, during the assault, one of them made a verbal threat that implicated both young men in Lizzie Wilson's murder.

> "CAUGHT. Willis Steptoe, colored, who, with Lewis Wadkins, attempted an outrage upon a white woman named Mays, at Ballehack, some time ago, has been captured, and is now in jail at Martinsville, Va. Deputy sheriff H.A. Webber left this (Thursday) morning for that place and will bring the villain here for trial. It is hoped and believed that his arrest will give some clue to the horrible murder of Miss Lizzie Wilson at Roanoke, last November, for it was Steptoe who made the threat that if his victim gave any alarm, 'he would do her like he did that girl in Roanoke.'"

This hearsay accusation from Miss Mays was enough to arrest Lewis Watkins at his home. Roanoke's Deputy Sheriff Henry Webber traveled 50 miles to the town of Martinsville, Virginia where Steptoe had been apprehended by local authorities. Webber brought his prisoner back to Roanoke in handcuffs to face charges.

A grand jury convened within a month and considered the flimsy evidence against the two young men. By the end of May 1885, Steptoe and Watkins were indicted for the murder of Lizzie Wilson. A trial date was set for July but, upon a motion from their defense counsel, postponed until later in the fall.

First, the two men stood trial for the attempted rape of Miss Mays. Their defense attorney, Henry Gibson, argued the case successfully. The jury voted for acquittal. Steptoe and Watkins walked out of one courtroom as innocent men, but their hands were still bound in chains. Soon they would face another trial before a jury, this time, for murder.

The Trials

On November 5, 1885 — a year and a day since Lizzie Wilson's murder — Steptoe and Watkins appeared in court. For 19th century rural Virginia, it was unusual for a trial to occur after such a long delay. Even for capital offenses, a defendant could typically be arrested, tried, sentenced, and executed within a few weeks of the crime.

Imagine the anxiety and apprehension felt by these two young men as they ascended the courthouse steps. All the symbols of the United States justice system loomed above their heads: the flag of stars and stripes, the Grecian columns and the tall windows. They stood before a wall of framed portraits and a judge's bench of impressive dark-colored woodwork. These architectural trappings combined with the angry spectators must have been intimidating and terrifying.

Their lives and their legal defense lay in the hands of two attorneys: Henry Gibson and John Allen Watts. Gibson had successfully defended Watkins and Steptoe in the previous case for attempted rape.

One wonders how the lawyers Gibson and Watts were paid for their services. At the time, the concept of a public defender did not exist. A few larger cities such as New York had non-profit charities or legal aid societies dedicated to providing assistance to the poor. However, the idea of public defense as counter-balance to a public prosecutor only gained traction in the early 20th century. The first true public defender office would be established in 1913 in Los Angeles, California. Which means that the legal team in this trial was likely paid by the families of Watkins and Steptoe fund-raising within their church-going community.

Henry Gibson, a young lawyer about 25 years old, came from the capital city Richmond, Virginia. His father was a prominent citizen who earned success as an insurance underwriter; the elder Mr. Gibson was secretary of the Virginia Underwriters Association. Henry Gibson graduated the University of Virginia and came to Roanoke in 1882 to open his law practice. He had an office on Commerce Street not far from the Roanoke city courthouse. In his personal life, he was no stranger to tragedy: his only brother and one sister died of childhood illnesses; his teenaged sister Susie had accidentally drowned the year before.

Gibson was a popular fellow in town, well-liked by his colleagues. Testimonials called him gifted, efficient, conscientious, and a character of integrity. His co-counsel J. Allen Watts spoke of him as "an eloquent speaker, a close reasoner, and every effort showed marks of continued improvement."[1] His future career seemed bright as a rising star in Roanoke's legal community. A few years later, when he suddenly dropped dead of a stroke in January 1890, the newspapers overflowed with expressive eulogies. "Bold, fearless and outspoken, he was ever ready to defend the right, and neither motives of policy, nor persuasion, nor threats could deter him from following any course upon which he had once determined. In every position, he could be relied on to do his whole duty, and his fellow citizens can point with pride to his example as a faithful officer, a fearless pleader, and a conscientious man."[2]

John Allen Watts joined Gibson as co-counsel in the Lizzie Wilson murder trial. At 30 years old, his law career also showed a promising future. He had served as legal counsel for the Norfolk & Western Railway company since 1881, dealing mainly with business contracts and

---

[1] *Roanoke Daily Times*, January 18, 1890
[2] *Roanoke Daily Times*, January 19, 1890

real estate deals. Defending two African-American men from felony murder charges was a stark departure from his area of expertise.

Watts had his own share of personal tragedy. His mother died in childbirth and, as an only child, he was raised by his aunt. His late father William Watts, a former colonel in the Confederate army, left to his only son the family's estate known as the Oaklands. Located in northwest Roanoke, the property had several acres of lawns, flower gardens, and willow trees. The family name and the sprawling property gave Watts some degree of prominence in the community but that weighed against the cost of servants and groundskeepers required to maintain the estate. Watts later sold the Oaklands in 1890 to an entrepreneur land developer and moved his family to a modest house in the city. His wife Gertrude was active in the women's suffrage movement and in 1914 served as first vice-president of the Equal Suffrage League of Virginia.

Watts had a reputation as a distinguished attorney, as eulogized by an associate after his death in 1904. "As a lawyer, he relied more upon principle than upon precedent of decided cases. His mind was clear, logical and fair, and his ability to arrive at the material points in any controversy, and to discard the immaterial, has never been excelled. All courts before which he appeared recognized his eminent quality of fairness..."[3]

We must only imagine the eloquent legal defense that these two young lawyers presented to the court on that cool November morning. Unfortunately, from my inquiries to local court clerks, the original records of the trial are not available. We only have the newspaper reports on the outcome. Transcripts of witness testimony, along with arguments of the prosecutor and the defense counsel, likely never existed. Nowadays we are used to the courtroom scene of a stenographer typing swiftly in the corner, on a peculiar specialized keyboard, to transcribe in real-time a verbatim account of everything that is said. Court reporters and stenographers were not in common practice at the time of Watkins and Steptoe standing trial. The National Shorthand Reporters Association (NSRA) would not be established in Chicago, Illinois for another 15 years after the Lizzie Wilson murder trials. The first modern stenotype machine was invented in 1911. Which means that, in 1885, there was no

---

[3] Quoted from the *Typed Records of Watts Family Tree*, Historical Society of Western Virginia

standard procedure for recording the testimony given at trial.

Each attorney would have kept his own private, confidential notes among the records of his law practice. When an attorney retired or passed away, all of those records could be lost. Courts kept records of trial proceedings but generally the information is a brief summary of the outcome. For this period of history, especially in rural Virginia, the newspapers are the best and only source.

===

According to the *Richmond Dispatch*, the trial concluded 10 days later and went to jury deliberations. Attorneys Gibson and Watts defended the two young men vigorously from the prosecutor's circumstantial accusations. Spectators in the courtroom burst into applause after Gibson made his closing arguments. The judge surely banged his gavel and called for order.

On either side of the courtroom, two families anxiously awaited the jury's decision. The victim's parents and siblings, with their friends and allies, hoped for a swift conviction. They yearned to feel closure and reach a conclusion to their year-long agony. Whether or not the evidence was circumstantial or hearsay, I imagine they just wanted someone—anyone—to hang for the crime. The prosecutor must have assured the Wilson family that there was strong evidence of guilt. However, the accused men also had families, friends and allies who had lived in the Big Lick and Roanoke area for generations. Everyone in their community knew the blacksmith's son, the barbershop owner's brother, and the co-worker from the tobacco factory. Emancipated people and their adult children, now second-class citizens in segregated Roanoke, hoped for the impartial scales of justice to tilt in their favor for the first time in their lives.

The jury came back deadlocked. The 12 men were unable to reach a verdict, most likely for the absence of any evidence that proved either man's guilt beyond a reasonable doubt. The accusation from Miss Mays, that Steptoe had threatened her, was not enough. Although the seven white men of the jury voted to convict, the five Black men voted for acquittal.

The judge declared a mistrial due to the hung jury. This meant that the defendants were not convicted, but neither were they acquitted or free. Newspaper editorials blazed with outrage, a good example being the *Staunton Spectator*, December 1, 1885, "…This decision, on the color line, is one of the worst signs of the times that we have seen, since it is impossible that it could have been the results, without bias, of a difference in judgment touching the guilt or innocence of the prisoner at the bar."

The prisoners had to be hustled out of town for fear of a lynch mob. Sheriff Webber hurriedly put them on an evening train bound for a nearby county. He did his job in following the law. Without a doubt, he saved their lives that night. Steptoe and Watkins made it safely to the jail in Wytheville, Virginia (about 80 miles inland to the west) to await their retrial.

===

A second jury was summoned from the county, according to *The Richmond Dispatch*, January 2, 1886, and a trial would be held under the jurisdiction of the Hustings Court.[4] The paper also reported that more than 100 witnesses were summoned. One has to wonder if the Wilson family was among those called to testify, if Lizzie's parents or siblings were put on display to weep out their grief before the court. The defense may have called on the accused men's family, friends, and fellow church-goers to testify to their character. With the scarcity

---

[4] Based on English law and carried over to colonial Virginia, the county-level hustings courts typically handled cases such as business contracts, debts, land deeds, and wills. When presided over by a judge, the Hustings Court had the powers of a Circuit Court.

of newspaper accounts and the absence of official trial transcripts, we will never know what happened within those courthouse walls.

Presiding over the court was Judge Wingfield Griffin, a widely respected young judge from the nearby town of Salem. Not quite forty years old, Judge Griffin had advanced quickly in his career—appointed to the Roanoke County Court only a year after passing the bar. He came from a prosperous and influential family; his older brothers, known as The Fighting Griffins, had earned distinction fighting for the Confederate army. Judge Griffin had been too young to join his brothers on the battlefield but as a teenager hurriedly donned a gray uniform in the final, desperate days of the war. Nonetheless, as a judge he had a reputation for having an even temperament and being a stickler for proper legal procedure.

The prosecutor Mr. Robert H. Woodrum represented the Commonwealth of Virginia. A fairly young man, not quite 30 years old, he was a graduate of Roanoke College. His father was also an attorney and a newspaper publisher. After studying law in the nearby town of Salem, he was the first attorney for the Commonwealth elected by the people of Roanoke.

Two attorneys served as defense counsel: J. Allen Watts (from the first trial) and Colonel George Woodson Hansbrough. A seasoned attorney at 57 years old, Hansbrough was a prominent local farmer and a Confederate veteran. To the modern eye, it seems curious for a former officer of the Confederacy to defend a pair of African-American men in court. Apparently, Hansbrough was a forward-thinking man dedicated to legal principles above all. He believed in the Constitution and the Fourteenth Amendment; no matter the identity of the persons on trial, he would ensure that they received the benefit of due process of law.

Again, the jury in the second trial was unable to render a verdict. According to the *Richmond Dispatch*, April 16, 1886, the hung jury divided on racial lines. All seven white men voted guilty but the five Black men voted to acquit. Judge Griffin granted a motion from the defense for a change in venue. The two prisoners were spirited away for their own safety once again. They reached a new jailhouse in the town of Lynchburg, Virginia. In the next upcoming term of the Corporation Court, Watkins and Steptoe would be re-tried for a third time.

===

The third trial began in Lynchburg, according to a brief mention in the *Alexandria Gazette*, November 9, 1886. Court convened with a new jury of three white men and nine Black men. Perhaps the prosecutor hoped that a jury pool from another town, who did not know the accused men or their neighbors personally, would be less biased in their sympathy for the defendants. The prosecution called Miss Mays as a witness to repeat her story of how Wilson Steptoe allegedly threatened her during an assault. Defense attorneys, who had heard this testimony before, must have easily disputed her credibility. After all, both men had been tried and acquitted of the attempted rape charges in her case.

A week later, on November 17, 1886, *the Staunton Spectator* reported that the jury was unable to agree. Watkins and Steptoe were discharged—neither guilty or innocent—for a third time. On the second anniversary of the horrific crime, no one had yet been brought to justice. Each trial attracted more public interest and the courtrooms were crowded for every day of testimony. Again, the jury divided on the color line: the Black jurors voted for acquittal and the white jurors unanimously voted for conviction.

===

The fourth trial was scheduled to begin in the Corporation Court in Lynchburg, Virginia. The *Richmond Dispatch*, February 18, 1887 reported that the defense filed a motion to continue and the trial was rescheduled until April. The article criticized the high cost of trials and mistrials as "phenomenal in the history of criminal prosecutions in Virginia." The prosecution called a list of 28 witnesses, likely carried over from the previous three trials. The witnesses were accumulating serious expenses for travel, lodging, food, and time away from their jobs. "Added to the jail fees, board, and transportation of prisoners to and from the jails of Wytheville, Salem, Liberty, and Lynchburg, in all of which they have been confined, together with the expenses of the necessary officers, the sum will much more than reach the aggregate of that at Lynchburg, and still the courts seem to be no nearer the solution of the problem of who murdered the unfortunate girl than when these everlasting trials began."

Subsequent newspaper accounts are scattered or missing, but apparently the defense would file another motion to postpone the trial until the first week of June. The jury once more failed to convict, except for this time the division was not entirely on racial lines. According to the *Salem Times-Register*, four white men voted to convict, whereas one white man joined with the seven Black men in voting for acquittal.

A small headline "Set Free At Last" in the *Connecticut Western News*, June 15, 1887, reports that Watkins and Steptoe had been released from custody on a *nolle prosequi* order issued in Lynchburg by the Attorney of the Commonwealth. *Nolle prosequi* is a Latin phrase meaning "will no longer prosecute" or a variation on the same. The prosecution invokes *nolle prosequi* when it has decided to discontinue a prosecution. The effect is to leave matters as if charges had never been filed. It is not the same as an acquittal, which would have prevented any further proceedings against a defendant on the same charges by the principle of double jeopardy. It leaves open the door for a renewed prosecution on the same charge if new evidence is discovered.

A blistering headline: <u>A Brutal Murder Unavenged – Watkins and Steptoe, Charged with the Murder of Lizzie Wilson, Released from Custody</u> appeared in the *Salem Times-Register* on June 10, 1887. The article is less a factual report than a highly biased editorial seething with outrage for the expensive cost of trials, the "time and annoyance" spent for such a disappointing outcome.

"…the most brutal murder that ever blackened the history of Roanoke remains unavenged." Four trials had resulted in a deadlocked jury each time.

In the summer of 1887, the pair of accused men walked free after two years of imprisonment without bail. Their freedom came at a cost to their health and their livelihood. These young men had spent two years unable to earn wages for a days' work, confined behind bars in infamously unsanitary conditions. After they emerged into the light of day, their lives could never go back to normal.

===

My efforts to trace Wilson Steptoe's movements have been inconclusive. A fellow of the same name appeared in the 1900 federal census as a single man renting a room in a boarding house on 10th Avenue in Roanoke. His family remained in town. One brother, Oliver Steptoe, owned a barbershop on Salem Avenue. Another brother worked as a janitor. If Wilson Steptoe moved frequently, did not own a home, or worked odd jobs as a laborer, he did not leave much of a paper trail behind. Whatever became of him after leaving the courthouse is lost to time.

Lewis Watkins continued living in Roanoke near his family but his freedom would be short-lived. Just four years later, on October 19, 1891, he died of consumption (tuberculosis) at his home on Sixth Avenue NW. A brief article in *The Roanoke Times* is not a sympathetic obituary but an opportunity to remind the readers of the crime. "Watkins was one of the negroes who were arrested for the murder of Lizzie Wilson in 1884. Wilson Steptoe was the other. They were tried several times, and strong evidence was introduced in each instance, but the colored members of the jury invariably held out that the prisoners were not guilty. As a consequence, the prisoners were finally released from custody."

Four trials in four different courthouses had failed to convict Steptoe and Watkins of the crime, but in the eyes of the public, their names would always be under suspicion.

===

One year after Watkins and Steptoe walked free out of court, a fellow named William Jones was lynched. Jones had been accused of assaulting a white woman named Mrs. Midkiff in Pulaski County, Virginia. The law enforcement officers attempted to safeguard the accused man from threats of extralegal violence by transporting him from a jail in Wytheville to the town of Lynchburg. Their efforts of quietly moving the prisoner in the dark of night were in vain.

About 25 vigilantes overwhelmed the sheriff and his two deputies at the depot. They forced the prisoner off the train and dragged him to a nearby tree to be hung. As they put a noose around his neck, the lynch mob apparently extracted a full confession from William Jones for the assault of which he was accused as well as a similar crime in Boone County, West Virginia.

The vigilantes later reported on their end-of-rope confession, saying "that he was the murderer of Lizzie Wilson, whose horrible death in Roanoke in 1884 is so well remembered by our readers. The negro said his right name was William Jones; that he cut Lizzie Wilson's throat with a razor, and then remained in Roanoke more than a month after the crime was committed. Jones said to the gentleman who gave us this information that the two men Mr. Henry Webber arrested for the murder of the girl were entirely innocent, and that no one had anything to do with it but himself. This information comes from a source that we regard as reliable, and thus the mystery of this horrible murder is solved."

This account was printed in the *Salem-Times Register* on July 13, 1888 with heavy-handed editorial bias, showing no sympathy or outrage for the murder of William Jones at the hands of a lawless lynch mob. The coerced confession was reported to the newspaper from an unnamed, so-called "gentleman who was a witness of the whole transaction, but not a participant." Hearsay from an anonymous source failed to carry weight with either the public or with Roanoke's sheriff. William Jones was never charged posthumously for Lizzie Wilson's murder and the mystery remains unsolved to this day.

The Lawman

Sheriff Charles Webber had only been in office for a year on the night Lizzie Wilson was murdered. Until that moment, his job involved containing the general disorder in the saloons, the brothels, and the rough parts of town. Bar fights, stabbings or pistol shootings in the street were not mysteries. Violent squabbles between two drunken men did not arouse community outrage. Lizzie's case was different for having no reliable eyewitnesses. There was no clear motive beyond a random, spontaneous assault. There was no evidence at the crime scene. Six months of investigation, under intense public scrutiny, resulted in arrests but only on circumstantial evidence. The prosecutor's case relied on Miss Mays's word against Watkins and Steptoe—her claims of attempted assault and her recollection of a threat. In many cases, under the unwritten "lynch law" the mere whisper of accusation would be enough to condemn the prisoners to death.

Lynching mania was a common atrocity in the South in the years following the Civil War and up through the civil rights movement of the 1950s. Tens of thousands of men, women, and children were butchered by lynch mobs and the Ku Klux Klan. As described by anti-lynching activist Ida B. Wells in a speech delivered in Chicago in 1900, "Our country's national crime is lynching. It is not the creature of an hour, the sudden outburst of uncontrolled fury, or the unspeakable brutality of an insane mob. It represents the cool, calculating deliberation of intelligent people who openly avow that there is an 'unwritten law' that justifies them in putting human beings to death without complaint under oath, without trial by jury, without opportunity to make defense, and without right of appeal."

Sheriff Webber clearly believed in the rule of law — not lynch law — and took seriously his oath to the badge he wore. He could have opened the jailhouse doors to the howling lynch mob, on the night of their arrest, or at any time after a trial failed to convict Watkins and Steptoe. Many other sheriffs across the southern states cooperated with lynch mobs, some even participating in the frenzy. Instead, he protected the prisoners in his care by putting them on the evening train out of town. He made sure that they stood in a courtroom before a judge and jury. He accepted the outcome when the two men walked free.

===

Sheriff Charles Webber did not begin his career as a law enforcement officer. As a youth in what is now West Virginia, he learned the printer's trade and established the first newspaper in Salem, *The Roanoke Times*, that he would later sell to his brother Frank. He transitioned into public service gradually, first as a justice of the peace, and then standing as a sergeant-at-arms in the Virginia senate.

He enlisted in the Confederate army in 1861 as soon as the war broke out. He joined the famous Stonewall brigade and was injured in a battle. He recovered from his wounds, returned to the front lines, and continued to serve up until the final surrender at Appomattox.

After the war, Charles Webber joined the short-lived Readjuster Party — a progressive, state-level political party that was formed in Virginia during the late 1870s. This small detail from his obituary gives some insight into the sheriff's point-of-view at the time of Lizzie Wilson's murder.

The Readjuster Party promoted education for African-Americans by refinancing Virginia's Civil War debt and investing in public schools. They abolished the poll tax (that disenfranchised voters who were unable to pay) and cruel punishments such as the public whipping post. Because of the Readjuster Party's support of expanded voting rights, the town of Danville, Virginia elected a Black-majority town council and hired a racially integrated police force.

The Readjusters won a legislative majority and briefly dominated the political landscape in Virginia for about 20 years. The party elected a governor, installed justices on the state Supreme Court, and sent its members to the U.S. Senate. The party's platform and values aligned with the Republican Party as it was then—the party of Abraham Lincoln and the federal union. A key figure in the Readjuster Party was William Mahone, a former Confederate general who was president of several railroads. Readjusters nominated judges to the Virginia Supreme Court from their ranks. They appointed the lawyer George W. Hansbrough (defense attorney at one of the Watkins and Steptoe trials) as the official reporter of judicial decisions.

In the mid-1880s, after the election of President Grover Cleveland, the Southern Democratic Party revitalized on so-called conservative principles and organized its efforts to oppose Readjuster candidates on all levels. Within a few years, the Democratic Party regained control of the state legislature. The Readjuster Party collapsed and dissolved in 1895, opening the doors for Virginia's dominant Democratic Party to embed "Jim Crow" laws into the Virginia Constitution.

Racial segregation laws had been adopted on a local level, but in the late 1890s became state law applied to public facilities including all schools and vehicles of transportation. Those with any African ancestry could no longer serve on juries or run for political office. Specifically in Roanoke, from 1911 to 1917, city ordinances required the two races to live apart, including a law that created segregation districts where Black people were required to live. Everything else outside of the Gainsborough neighborhood, and a district to its north, was designated "whites-only."

===

Charles Webber was elected sheriff initially on the Readjuster ticket and four years later, after the Readjuster Party collapsed, he campaigned as a Republican. Never again did he return to the southern Democratic Party. Near the end of his second term as sheriff, in May 1891, Charles Webber chose not to run for reelection claiming failing health. His resignation cleared the field for a Democratic nominee George William Zirkle.

Sheriff Charles Webber's life came to a tragic end in August 1896 when he committed suicide. *The Roanoke Daily Times*, August 8, 1896, reported on the incident in graphic detail, how he was found at home in bed with a pistol in his hand. He shot himself in the head.

The newspaper printed a lengthy biography of the former sheriff, clearly written in collaboration with friends and family members. Webber was said to be under the influence of opiates "a great deal recently" and the article presumes that the opioid addiction influenced his suicidal thoughts. For about a year prior to his death, Webber had been an invalid and seldom seen outside his home.

===

Henry Webber, the sheriff's younger brother, served Roanoke as deputy sheriff. Far from simply overseeing the city jail, Henry Webber acted as a detective and conducted relentless investigations. The evidence that he collected built the case against Watkins and

Steptoe for the murder of Lizzie Wilson, but failed to prove their guilt beyond the shadow of a doubt.

Years later, in 1891, he would successfully track down another high-profile murder suspect. Ironically it would be an un-related fellow named Watkins accused of murdering his own wife to pursue an affair with another woman. (Given the large number of persons named Watkins, this appears to be a coincidence and not a relative of the man accused of Lizzie Wilson's murder.) The second of Roanoke's sensational murder cases had a very different outcome with actual evidence, several witnesses including those of his own extended family, and an un-coerced jailhouse confession before walking to the gallows. The judicial execution of Charles Watkins left no unsolved mystery behind, unlike the tragedy of Lizzie Wilson that no doubt continued to haunt Henry Webber every day.

In his personal life, Deputy Sheriff Henry Webber had more than his share of tragedy. He lost two wives from complications of childbirth and buried five of his nine children before they reached the age of two—all within a span of ten years. Solving the murder committed by Charles Watkins was the last case that Henry Webber worked on. His health failed later that year. In December 1891, at the age of 43, he passed away quietly at home.

The Parents

"We should never have come here," Mrs. Wilson may have said to her husband John after the violent murder of their 14-year-old daughter. The crime was senseless and horrific. After the initial trauma of discovering the corpse and completing the funeral arrangements, this mother was left to carry the burden of emotions. Anger, terror, sorrow, frustration, helplessness, confusion, self-blame or blaming others — any or all of these could have overwhelmed the woman who had endured so much. She may have blamed her husband for bringing the family to such a dangerous place. Worst of all, this mother could have subconsciously blamed Lizzie the victim for contributing to her own murder. The newspapers reprinted the same story: that Lizzie chose to separate from her sister, that she took a short-cut across a vacant field, that she laughed recklessly into the darkness where evil lurked. Compounding the agony of her grief, the same phrases, "if only Lizzie had been more careful…" or, "if only we had never come to Roanoke…" may have kept replaying in Mrs. Wilson's thoughts.

===

At the time of her teenage daughter's murder, Elizabeth Jane Wilson had brought nine healthy children into the world, nourished them and ferociously protected them. In those days of high infant mortality, it was a triumph for all of her children to survive into adulthood. To have one of her daughters snatched away was unbearable after all the hardships this mother had endured to hold the family together.

From the beginning, Mrs. Wilson's life had not been an easy one. Her father George Edwards was a sawyer working at a lumber mill on the river near Godalming, in Surrey, just west of London. If the records I have uncovered are the right ones (and not persons of a similar name) then her christening in September 1844 occurred only two months after her parents' marriage in July. In other words, her mother Caroline (Webster) Edwards was already pregnant at the wedding. This either means that George Edwards married Caroline to give legitimacy to his own child, or he married a desperate woman carrying another man's child.

As a teenaged girl of 16, she lived apart from her parents in the household of her mother's sister Mary. In the England census of 1861, young Elizabeth Edwards was listed as a "servant" for Mr. John Kendall and his wife Mary. They lived in the town of Wateringbury, in the county of Kent, southeast of London and about 60 miles away from her hometown in Godalming.

Her uncle John Kendall had married her mother's sister Mary Webster in November 1852 and after 10 years had three children. John Kendall was the headmaster of the National School and his wife Mary assisted him as the school's headmistress. Clearly, it was Elizabeth's duty to care for the young children and perform menial household chores.

Elizabeth's parents stayed in Godalming with her four younger brothers and sisters. George Edwards continued to work at the lumber mill — an occupation that his son Henry would follow someday. From what I have gathered, the list of Elizabeth's siblings shows a close similarity to the names of her own children: Georgiana, Emily, Ann, and Henry. Naming one's children after close relatives is a way to honor their memory or maintain a bond across the generations. Perhaps she missed her siblings left behind and a childhood cut short by economic necessity. She worked from a young age as a nanny and transitioned straight into married life.

===

John Satchell Wilson, a brick mason about 10 years older, offered Elizabeth Edwards a life beyond servitude. He was by no means a wealthy man but he had a steady occupation, a supportive network of the Masonic brotherhood, and the fearless optimism of a building contractor always hunting for the next job. For myself as a researcher, uncovering the origins of John Satchell Wilson in England, despite the tell-tale middle name, has been a nearly insurmountable ordeal.

John Wilson married Elizabeth Jane Edwards on Christmas Day 1863 in a town called Chertsey, in Surrey County, England. Their marriage certificate records his father's name as Charles Wilson, who was also a bricklayer. John was born in Rugby, Warwickshire in the mid-1830s but prior to July 1837 when England passed a law to require the national registration of births and deaths. The only hope of finding an official record of his christening would be to dive into a sea of Wilsons in the local parish church registers, many of which are not digitized or indexed.

From the beginning of their marriage, they moved from town to town, from one construction project to the next. According to birth records from England, she bore their first child Harry George Wilson on October 19, 1864 in the town of Hoxton, Middlesex. Their second child Caroline Alice was born on September 21, 1866 in Deptford, Kent. They moved to the town of Colney Hatch, Middlesex, where she delivered two more children on a schedule of approximately every two years: William on March 3, 1868 and her namesake Elizabeth Jane on August 28, 1870. The fifth child Annie (born in 1872 or 1873) was a swaddling baby when John Wilson decided to immigrate to North America.

===

One reason for leaving England could have been financial hardship. The 1870s was a period of economic downturn and upheaval. Following the end of the Civil War in America in 1865, and the decade of Reconstruction, the United States emerged as an industrial manufacturer and threatened to become a substantive economic rival of Europe. Then, after the Franco-Prussian War ended in 1871, a newly-unified Germany ascended to a powerful position that subordinated other European nations such as France and Austria-Hungary. A global financial crash called the Panic of 1873 caused a chain-reaction of bank failures and temporarily closed the New York stock exchange.

Another reason for leaving England was much more personal. Elizabeth Wilson's mother Caroline Edwards was admitted for "acute melancholia" to the Brookwood Asylum, in Woking, Surrey, in late September 1872. She died within a few days of entering the asylum. Perhaps she had suffered from mental illness for many years. It is too much of a coincidence that the Wilsons' residence in Friern Barnet (since the late 1860s) was nearby another mental institution, the Colney Hatch Lunatic Asylum.

Mrs. Wilson's siblings stayed behind in England when she departed for North America. Her brother Henry Edwards continued to work at the local saw mill, like his father before him, and lived in Godalming, Surrey. Her three sisters (Ann, Georgiana, and Emily) worked as household servants until they found husbands for themselves. Her aunt Mary and her uncle John Kendall moved to the county of Gloucestershire and continued working as schoolmasters until their retirement.

As far as I know, Mrs. Wilson never saw her siblings, her aunt and uncle, or her cousins ever again.

===

John Wilson apparently travelled alone to Canada a few months ahead of his family to make the necessary arrangements. Perhaps he accompanied a group of his fellow brick masons. An offer of employment may have lured him to seek his fortune on a foreign shore. Canada had recently subdivided in 1867 its provinces of Nova Scotia, New Brunswick, Quebec, and Ontario. New opportunities beckoned, especially in Ontario that enjoyed booming growth in manufacturing and financial sectors, industries and transportation networks. By the end of the 19th century, Ontario vied with Quebec as the nation's leader in terms of growth in population, industry, arts, and communications.

When her husband gave the word that a better home was waiting for them in the new land, Mrs. Wilson alone packed up her household and transported her five children to North America. First, she rode a train north to the port city of Liverpool and bought tickets for the popular Allan Line of passenger ships. Like the majority of emigrants of the time, it is doubtful that the Wilsons had the means to afford cabin-class accommodations. This means that Mrs. Wilson and her five small children likely travelled in steerage class.

On a Thursday evening, October 9, 1873, she melded into the crowd of passengers walking up the ramp from the wharf to the deck of the steamship. She held baby Annie in her arms and four small children tagged behind her skirts. They slept in steerage quarters that had been converted from cargo spaces. This area of the ship was dark, crowded and close to the water line. During the day, the passengers could get fresh air on the main deck. At night, or when seas were rough, the passengers were confined in the poorly ventilated space. Steerage passengers were further separated into single men, married couples and children, while single women were strictly segregated from all other passengers. Steerage quarters had berths lining the walls and a dining space in the middle where passengers cooked, ate, and washed together. They passed the hours by playing card games, sewing, or writing in journals.

My father recalled a family anecdote of the Wilsons' voyage across the Atlantic Ocean. The baby developed a high fever while they were at sea. Mrs. Wilson feared the captain would toss a sick baby overboard to avoid infecting the rest of the passengers. The story goes that she kept her baby quietly hidden below decks and, somehow, evaded the captain's merciless eye.

The passenger list of the steamship *Caspian* shows their arrival in the port of Quebec City on Monday,

October 20, 1873 after 12 days at sea. The list gives the names and ages of her children: Harry is 9, Alice is 6, William is 5, Elizabeth is 3, and Annie is an infant.

===

The Wilsons lived in Stratford, Ontario for about five years and had two more children: Georgiana Emily and Albert Edward. The Wilsons would have felt very much at home in this quaint, developing town in eastern Canada. Stratford's population was primarily made of immigrants from England, Ireland, and Scotland in contrast to the adjacent province of Quebec that attracted immigrants from France. The town and the nearby river were named after Stratford-upon-Avon, England, the birthplace of William Shakespeare.

How different their lives would have been if they had stayed in Stratford, Ontario. John Wilson made a choice, for whatever reason I do not know, to leave Canada for the United States. Most likely, Mr. Wilson learned of a better job opportunity from an advertisement or from one of his Freemason brothers. At some point in between Albert's birth in January 1878 and my grandmother Isabelle's birth in August 1880, Mrs. Wilson packed up her household and all seven children. They made a short journey to the south, across Lake Erie, and settled in the port city of Cleveland, Ohio.

Unless I can find an obscure record of either their ferry tickets or train tickets, there are no official records of the Wilsons' immigration from Canada to the United States. They arrived about 10 years before the Immigration Act of 1891 that gave the federal government direct control of inspecting all foreign travelers seeking admission to the United States. The 1891 Act expanded the list of excludable classes, barring the immigration of persons convicted of crimes of moral turpitude and those suffering contagious diseases. In January 1892, the Immigration Service opened the best known immigrant processing station on Ellis Island in New York Harbor. Until that time, immigrants of European descent had no restrictions.

===

The 1880 federal census of Cleveland, Ohio lists John Wilson a brick mason, his wife Elizabeth, and their seven children: Harry, Alice, William, Elizabeth, Annie, Georgiana, and Albert. My grandmother, Isabelle Marie, does not appear on the census record because it was enumerated on June 11, 1880—just two months before her ch on the 13th of August. Except for the eldest son Harry, the younger children all attended school.

The family lived at 371 Union Avenue in the southeast part of Cleveland, in a neighborhood that would later be dubbed Union-Miles Park. This area attracted a large number of Irish, Scottish, English and Welsh immigrants in the second half of the 19th century to work in the steel industry. The neighborhood was known as "Irishtown."

The eldest son Harry Wilson, at age 15, worked at the Cleveland Rolling Mill. Teenaged Harry would have labored hard, long days of boiler plate, steel wire and railroad-related manufacturing under the noxious clouds of smokestacks. At the time, Cleveland was the nation's second-largest producer of iron (second only to Pennsylvania) and by 1880, Cleveland's economy was dominated by the iron and steel industry. Living in the shadow of the steel mills meant enduring the noise of city trolleys, air pollution, and glare from the blast furnaces that lit up the night sky.

Perhaps the Wilsons would have continued to endure life in the steel town if not for the labor riots that occurred in the summer of 1882. The union of Amalgamated Association of Iron & Steel Workers demanded a "closed shop" that would restrict the employer from hiring or employing non-union workers. By comparison, an "open shop" does not require union membership of potential or current employees. The union also demanded a fixed wage scale.

When the union demands were rejected by the Cleveland Rolling Mill's president William Chisholm, the workers walked off the job. Briefly, the steel mills ceased operations. Chisholm brought in large numbers of Polish and Czech workers as strikebreakers. On Monday, June 5, 1882, the rolling mill reopened its operations. Violence erupted the following week, as the strikers threw rocks at the replacement workers who crossed the picket lines. Public sympathy turned away from the union because of their violent tactics. The city's officials supported the company against the striking laborers. Local police called in reinforcements to maintain order. After several weeks, the union was unable to gain support for the strike from the newly hired eastern European workers.

By the end of July 1882, the strike collapsed. Most of the Irish, Welsh and English workers never returned to their jobs at the steel mill. Unemployed, a majority of the immigrants from the British Isles chose to leave Cleveland and go elsewhere. In the summer of 1882, John Wilson decided to shop around for a new place to raise his ever-growing family. As always, he searched for new opportunities that promised a better life.

===

Once again and for the last time, Mrs. Wilson left a home behind. She travelled by train from Cleveland, Ohio to the Shenandoah Valley in Virginia, following her husband's pursuit of greener pastures. Her youngest daughter Sadie was about one year old and just learning to walk. My grandmother, Isabelle Marie, was a toddler. The older children (Alice, William, Elizabeth, Annie, Georgiana, and Albert) had to carry their own weight.

The first-born son Harry George Wilson turned 18 years old when the Wilsons moved to Roanoke. It appears he did not accompany the family to Virginia but went directly from Ohio to either New York or Maryland where he would meet his future wife. Harry lived apart from the rest of the Wilsons, making his own way in the world and tending to the needs of his own family. Later, he would have learned the news of his little sister's murder from the newspapers.

The family's dreams of a better life were shattered by what happened to Lizzie, not only the murder itself but the agony of never finding closure. The Wilsons endured lifelong uncertainty of never finding who did the terrible deed beyond a shadow of a doubt. They never saw her killer brought to justice.

Mrs. Wilson delivered her tenth and last child, Walter Scott Wilson, in October 1889 just five years after Lizzie's murder. She was a woman in her early forties, and it was somewhat unusual to still be having babies at that age. Perhaps she hoped that one more child would help to heal her soul after losing another.

===

However, Lizzie was not the only member of the family who fell victim to a violent crime in Roanoke. Almost 10 years later, her younger brother Albert was stabbed at random by a knife-wielding boy. *The Roanoke Times*, Tuesday, May 16, 1893, reported on the incident in great detail. "A Young Tramp's Crime: Albert Wilson Stabbed and Dangerously Wounded Sunday." The incident began on a Sunday afternoon when 15-year-old Albert Wilson (along with two friends) went in search of his father's wayward cow. The search led the boys to the rock quarry in the eastern part of the city. They encountered a youth named Robert Early who appeared to be drunk. Early flourished a barlow knife and declared that he would cut the first boy he met. Albert broke into a run but did not manage to escape Robert Early and his gang of ruffians. In the scuffle that followed, Albert received a stab wound to the left shoulder.

Some men who were passing by came to his assistance. Upon removing Albert's coat, they discovered that the wound was bleeding profusely. The men helped to carry him home to his frantic mother. A doctor arrived just in time to save Albert from bleeding to death and advised that the lung may have been penetrated.

Police quickly arrested what the newspaper called a "gang of tramps" known to be loitering in the area. The assailant's father John Early, along with three others, were fined $10 each and consigned to hard labor on a chain gang. The knife-wielding boy Robert Early was described as "a very repulsive-looking, unprepossessing youngster." Although he was a juvenile, Early appeared in court alone to answer for his crime. A grand jury quickly sent the boy to trial and punishment.

Once again, the Wilson family's unwanted celebrity status put a bookend on this newspaper story. "Albert Wilson, the victim of this unfortunate affair is a brother of Lizzie Wilson, whose mysterious and tragic death on the evening of the Presidential election in 1884 near where the Bridge Works now stands[5], is still fresh in the minds of the people of Roanoke."

It bears mentioning the obvious, that because Albert's assailants were white (not African-American) they were given due process of law. The courts levied fines and sentenced the men to a chain gang. At no point did blood-thirsty mobs surround the jailhouse crying for vengeance on behalf of Lizzie's brother. No one dragged the so-called "gang of tramps" into the streets to be executed without a trial. This incident is a sharp contrast to Roanoke's infamous lynching riot that would erupt in the streets just four months later.

===

The last time the Wilson family appears together in an official record is the 1900 federal census of Roanoke, Virginia. John Wilson, age 42, a bricklayer born in England, lived at 432 Seventh Avenue N.E. with his wife "Jane" and three children at home. Albert, now a single man aged 21, worked as a coach painter for the railway shops. The youngest teenaged daughter, Sadie, attended school as did her 10-year-old brother Walter Scott Wilson.

---

[5] The facilities and machine shops of the Virginia Bridge & Iron Company were once located at the east end of Madison Avenue near 9th Street N.E.

Mrs. Elizabeth Jane Wilson passed away just five months after the census-taker knocked on her door. Ironically, her death on November 3, 1900 was the eve of yet another grim anniversary of Lizzie's murder. After enduring 16 years of grief for her daughter, one might say this mother died of a broken heart. Her obituary "Death of Mrs. Wilson" in the *Roanoke Times*, November 4, 1900 reports that she died of heart failure on the previous morning. Her health had been failing for several weeks and her passing did not come as a surprise.

The obituary lists all of her surviving children: four sons and five daughters. Cryptically, the newspaper mentions that "with the exception of one son" all of Mrs. Wilson's children were present at her bedside. Her funeral was held at St. John's Episcopal church. She is buried in the City Cemetery on Tazewell Avenue near the tomb of her beloved lost daughter Lizzie.

John Satchell Wilson continued living in Roanoke as a widower for the next 10 years. As he grew older and was no longer able to work as a bricklayer, he may have relied on the financial support of his Masonic Lodge brotherhood and his adult children. He reflected with pride on his many accomplishments of participating in the construction development of the Magic City. As a bricklayer and mason, John Wilson had a hand in the Hotel Roanoke's construction and renovations, the buildings of Hollins College, and many other projects.

Shortly before his death, the 1910 federal census shows John Wilson living alone, renting a room in a boardinghouse at 375 Salem Avenue NW a few blocks from the downtown railroad depot.

===

I know of just one person in John Wilson's extended family. A younger brother George Satchell Wilson stayed behind in England. He worked as a building contractor for most of his life and travelled the world (Argentina, Peru, and South Africa) to participate in construction projects. In the 1870s, around the same time that John Wilson brought his family to Canada, George Wilson made a brief sojourn to the foreign-backed developments in South America. He stayed long enough for his oldest son Arthur Satchell Wilson to be born in Lima, the capital city of Peru.

After the birth of his third child, George Wilson settled down in Hanwell, England, a suburb of west London. He built two adjacent homes on Uxbridge Road and for a few years lived side-by-side with his eldest son Arthur.

George S. Wilson visited the United States for the first and only time in the spring of 1905, at the age of 66, for the stated purpose of "visiting brother John Wilson in Roanoke, Virginia." According to the ship's passenger records, he boarded a steamship in Liverpool on May 13, 1905 and arrived at Ellis Island, New York on May 21, 1905. George S. Wilson visited Virginia to reunite with his brother after 30 years of separation. He met his nieces and nephews in Roanoke and stayed for about a month to enjoy the scenery of rural Virginia. The *Roanoke Times* mentions his visit in the society column as if he were a celebrity. The paper called him "one of London's largest sewerage contractors" and reports that he departed June 28, 1905 to return home.

Along his journey from New York to Virginia, he had made a brief detour. George Wilson stopped in Washington D.C. to visit the eldest of the Wilson children. The *Washington Times* society column reported, on May 28, 1905: "George Wilson, of Kent, England, is visiting his nephew Harry G. Wilson, 351 I Street southwest." Perhaps the two men discussed their mutual business interests in real estate and building construction.

As a footnote to this episode, three months later, the society column of the *Evening Star* newspaper of Washington D.C. reports this tidbit: "Mr. George E. Wilson and sister, Miss Myrtle, pupils of Central High School, eldest son and daughter of Harry G. Wilson, a well-known local contractor, sailed Wednesday on the steamer Oceanic for England, where they will spend the remainder of the summer with their uncle."

===

John Wilson died alone on a Saturday afternoon, May 28, 1910 at the age of 74. A quiet funeral was held on the evening of May 30 at the home of his son Albert E. Wilson, 706 Stewart Avenue. He is buried in the City Cemetery together with his wife and daughter.

The obituary printed in the *Evening News*, May 30, 1910, makes brief mention of his passing away, then spends more than two-thirds of the article rehashing the circumstances of a sensational crime from over 25 years before. "The death of Mr. Wilson revives memories of the sad death of Miss Lizzie Wilson, his daughter, who was brutally murdered… To this day, the murder is one of the unsolved mysteries of the police department." Whatever John Wilson's life had been for seven decades, in the end, he was known to the public for only one thing — being the father of the murdered girl.

The Siblings

The nine sisters and brothers of Lizzie Wilson shared the tragic bond of being related to the famous murdered girl. The older ones suffered the lifelong trauma of witnessing the event. Vivid memories of that night cast a shadow over every day of the rest of their lives. The younger ones carried dim childhood memories or only knew the story second-hand. They suffered the trauma passed down from their elders, a burden to carry that they did not quite understand.

Some of them stayed in Roanoke while others pursued their dreams elsewhere. Throughout the years, they remained close and travelled often to see each other. The local newspapers reported on visitors coming and going, in what appears to the modern eye to be an intrusive journalist loitering at the train depot. At times, they shared rooms in each other's homes when they fell on hard times. My father benefitted from this custom of family hospitality when he embarked into the world as a young man. In the 1940 census of Washington D.C., my father (in his twenties) worked as a clerk in a drug store while living in the home of his Aunt Georgiana with his cousins Maude and Harry Lyles.

As the years rolled on, the Wilson siblings managed to put the darkness of the past behind them. Most of them lived well into their 70s and 80s, enjoyed long stable marriages, and raised families of their own. Their sister's murder was a defining moment for the family but, ultimately, it did not define them.

#

The eldest son **Harry George Wilson** (1864 – 1948) never spent a day living in Roanoke with the rest of the family. He embarked out of Cleveland, Ohio as soon as he turned 18 and never looked back. He married in December 1885 to Miss Margaret Newman, a native of Maryland and a descendent of Revolutionary War patriots. Their first son George Edward Wilson was born in Troy, New York within the first year of marriage. Their two other children, Myrtle and Harry, were born in Washington D.C.

Harry G. Wilson enjoyed a classic rags-to-riches success story. He was a self-made man, rising above his working-class origins to a position of status and prosperity. He wisely invested in undeveloped land in the suburbs of Maryland and the District of Columbia at the turn of the century. In the 1910s and 1920s, as the modern-day capitol buildings and monuments were being renovated, that area turned into profitable real estate.

Harry served as Vice-President of the Metropolis Building & Loan Association in D.C. as early as 1917 and continued his involvement with that organization for the rest of his life. The early newspapers from the Gilded Era are full of his children entertaining at high-society activities, including detailed descriptions of his daughter Myrtle's fashionable attire. One of his sons attended Cornell University and his other son attended the University of Virginia.

At Harry and Margaret's lavish 25th wedding anniversary celebration in 1910, a string orchestra performed among Christmas decorations and American Beauty roses. Years later, during the Great Depression of the 1930s, they had a more subdued celebration for their Golden 50th anniversary. Harry died at the age of 84 and is buried with his wife in Cedar Hill Cemetery in Prince George's County, Maryland.

===

The eldest daughter **Caroline Alice Wilson** (1866 - 1958) accompanied the family from Cleveland to Roanoke and remained there for her entire adult life. At 18 years old, she witnessed her sister's murder and stood by her mother's side through the anguished years that followed.

I imagine she stepped into the role of the steady, dependable one who supported her parents until the end. As is common in large families, Alice as the eldest girl served as a second maternal figure to her many younger siblings.

In the early 1890s, she married Samuel Dickinson who also was an immigrant from England. He made his living as a butcher. Later, he worked as a custodian of the Masonic Temple, perhaps alongside Alice's father. They had one daughter named Maude.

The Dickinsons lived together on 1411 Chapman Avenue in the more upscale, southwest part of town. They appeared to make extra income by renting out rooms to boarders. Their home had all the modern conveniences such as electricity, as the *Roanoke Times* reported in 1907 an incident where Alice received a severe shock when turning off a light in the kitchen.

After the turn of the century, Alice became active with the Ladies Aid Society of the West End Presbyterian church. The newspapers showcase a number of charity events and garden parties. For example, at a Valentine's Day tea party in 1912, Alice poured hot chocolate while her daughter and other young ladies wearing white dresses trimmed in red hearts served as hostesses. In June

1914, the Ladies Aid Society hosted a fundraiser at the church where they sold ice cream, cake, and candy.

Their marriage lasted more than four decades. Samuel Dickinson died at the age of 77 during the Great Depression of the 1930s. Alice lived on as a widow for another 20 years until she died at the age of 92. Of all her siblings, she lived the longest life.

===

The second son **William Wilson** (1868 – 1912) has been nearly impossible to trace in the years following his sister Lizzie's murder. The name is all too common, and family anecdotes about his life have been lost over the years. Anything could have happened to William after that fateful night when he heard his sister's screams and he rushed outside into the dark.

One theory is that he might have suffered a nervous breakdown over the guilt of being unable to protect his little sister and entered a mental institution. In those days, seeking mental health treatment carried a stigma. The so-called sanitariums or asylums, with their brick walls, padded rooms, and straight-jackets, kept their own private records of patient admissions. Those who died while in their care might be buried anonymously on the facility's grounds. If an institution shut down, its internal records were often sealed or lost.

He could have become an alcoholic, an opium addict, or a convicted felon sentenced to jail. Chasing down this possibility would involve more digging to weed out fellows with a similar name. On the brighter side, perhaps he enlisted in the military to fight the 1898 Spanish-America War. He could have traveled to Cuba, Puerto Rico, or the Philippines to participate in that year-long conflict.

Alternatively, he may have become a merchant sailor and found solace working on the open waters of the Atlantic Ocean. I found two newspaper articles that may or may not be the William Wilson that I seek. If these two articles involve the same person, he was a very unlucky fellow. The *Roanoke Daily Times* reported on March 10, 1890 that a William Wilson had been rescued with another man after five days on a small boat. They belonged to a fishing schooner and went adrift while attending trawls near Gloucester, Massachusetts. In the following year, September 16, 1891, the *Roanoke Times* reported on a fire that destroyed a six-story building in New York City. Among those hurt in fleeing the blaze was a fellow named

William Wilson, "a sailor, who injured his ankle while dropping from the fire escape."

After many frustrating years of sifting through lists of William Wilsons, I have found only two verified clues. First, his mother's obituary, printed in November 1900, mentioned that he lived somewhere in New York. The obituary also mentions cryptically that "all of her children, with the exception of one son, were present at her bedside" when Mrs. Wilson passed away. There is a one in four chance that William is the one who failed to appear at his mother's deathbed. Second, he died sometime prior to April 1912 according to a brief mention in The *Berkshire Eagle* newspaper of Pittsfield, Massachusetts, April 12, 1912: "Mrs. Abram [sic] Robarge and her brother Walter Wilson of this city received news last night of the death of their brother, William Wilson, of Catskill, N.Y. and they left last night for Catskill, N.Y." The town of Catskill, New York lies about 50 miles inland to the southwest of Pittsfield, Massachusetts. My inquiry to the county clerk of Catskill received a reply of "no record found" which only deepens the mystery.

I have a tattered, fading group photograph that includes my grandmother Isabelle (Wilson) Robarge standing with her brother Walter Scott Wilson and her sister Annie Garland. The back of the photograph is labeled simply "1912" as if for the person who noted the date needed no other explanation. They are not posing for a happy occasion. Now I understand that they are gathered together for a funeral.

===

Annie Maria Wilson (1872 – 1955) came to North America from England as a swaddling baby. After Lizzie's murder, the mother of the house became excessively strict and over-protective of her surviving daughters. Annie may have heard repeatedly the family anecdote of Mrs. Wilson's harrowing ocean trip from England to Canada, when the frantic mother concealed Annie the fever-stricken infant for fear of the steamship captain throwing a sick baby overboard.

When Annie was 18 years old, she showed her rebellious streak in her engagement to marry John Charles Garland. Originally, a wedding was planned for the middle of September but Mrs. Wilson began to raise "strenuous objections" to the marriage. The *Roanoke Times*, Sunday, August 9, 1891, reported the whole story of the "Runaway Match," how Annie evaded her mother's watchful eye and eloped.

An unnamed married lady played co-conspirator in the elopement scheme. She sent a messenger to ask Mrs. Wilson to visit a sick neighbor. While Mrs. Wilson's attention was occupied at the front door, Annie tip-toed out the back door with her suitcase. A group of friends accompanied Annie to the train station where they joined Mr. Garland. The wedding party rode the overnight train to Bristol, a city to the west that straddles the Virginia-Tennessee border. The couple hastily acquired a license and were married the same day. They returned to Roanoke on Saturday to the outrage of Annie's mother and the congratulations of their friends.

The Garlands had their first child, Edith, within the first year of their marriage. Their son James was born two years later. They relocated north to Pittsfield, Massachusetts where they had a third child John Charles Garland, Jr. By the time of the 1900 federal census, Annie's younger sister Isabelle (my grandmother) joined her in Pittsfield and stayed in the Garlands' home for a short time. Within 10 years, the family moved to Portsmouth, Virginia where they had their fourth child, George Wilson Garland.

Annie's husband Charles Garland worked as a machinist at the Norfolk Naval Shipyard for the next several decades, all through the expansion of that facility in World War I, until he retired in the 1930s. Their marriage lasted five decades until Charles Garland died in 1943 at age 74 of a heart attack. Annie lived on as a widow until she died in 1955 at the age of 82.

===

Georgiana Emily Wilson (1875 - 1942) was nine years old at the time of Lizzie's murder. At that age, she was old enough to understand what happened but not quite old enough to process the hailstorm of grief and rage that battered the family for years to come.

Prior to her mother's death, Georgiana left Roanoke as a single young woman. She followed her sister Annie Garland north to New England and, for a time, worked on the production line in a garment factory. In June 1902, she married Arthur Lambert Lyles in Pittsfield, Massachusetts. Most likely, Georgiana quit her job after she married. Her mother-in-law died in April 1910, and her father-in-law died in the fall of the same year. Arthur Lyles decided to move his family to Alexandria, Virginia that November and took ownership of his late father's shoe store.

At some point between 1920 and 1930, their marriage had apparently broken. I have not found a record if they were officially divorced or simply lived apart. On October 6, 1925, Georgiana enlisted the aid of her older sister Alice Dickinson, in Roanoke, to sign an affidavit that she had personal knowledge of the date and circumstances of Georgiana's birth. This signed declaration was filed with the Province of Ontario, Canada for Georgiana to obtain a delayed registration birth certificate. The purpose for obtaining this document could have been Georgiana applying for naturalization as a U.S. citizen (to vote) or it may have involved her efforts to legally separate from her husband.

The 1930 census shows an Arthur Lyles of the correct age (61) living alone in Alexandria, Virginia. At the same time Georgiana and her daughters Maude and Marian were living in Washington D.C. In the 1930 census, Georgiana lists her marital status as "widowed" which is technically untrue; in those days, it was a public disgrace for a woman to be divorced. Ironically, Arthur Lyles died in late April 1930, about two weeks after the census was taken.

Georgiana Lyles lived on as a widow for another 12 years. As mentioned in a previous chapter, my father Woodrow Wilson Robarge briefly lived in her home with his cousins as a young man starting off in the world. He affectionately called her "Aunt Dord" and perhaps his camera took the only photograph that I have of her.

At the age of 66, in September 1942, she passed away at home. Her daughter Maude Lyles and her son Harry Lyles survived her; the other daughter Marian had earlier died in childbirth in August 1940.

===

Albert Edward Wilson (1878 – 1934) was the third son in this large family of mostly girls. He was not quite seven years old when his older sister Lizzie was murdered. One wonders if he remembered her at all as a vague silhouette of layered skirts and pinned-up curls.

Albert spent his entire life in Roanoke—the only one of the Wilson boys to stay in the "Magic City" until the end. He worked for the Norfolk & Western Railway shops as a coach painter. One can imagine that he spent his days inhaling toxic paint fumes to stencil and paint freight cars. As he gained experience, he advanced to become the foreman of the railway car painting team. Apparently, he suffered from chronic ill health. He claimed a medical exemption for a hernia on his World War I military draft registration card.

He married twice, first in 1901 to a widow named Clara Wigginton who brought three teenaged children from her previous marriage. As far as I know, Albert never fathered any children of his own. Albert and Clara appear together as a couple in the 1910 and 1920 census of Roanoke, Virginia. They lived at 706 Stewart Avenue S.E. not far from the cemetery where his sister Lizzie was buried. In this modest home, Albert hosted the memorial service of his late father and arranged for John Wilson's burial.

In the mid-1920s, Albert and Clara shared a home with his younger sister Sadie and her husband on 1204 Patterson Avenue SW — a couple of city blocks away from the home of their sister Alice Dickinson on 1411 Chapman Avenue. Albert's wife Clara died in 1928 at the age of 63. In the 1930 census, I found Albert still living with his sister Sadie. He did not stay a widower for very long. He married again in 1932 to a younger woman, Hazel Hallsey, who had previously rented a room at his sister Alice's house. One wonders if he met his second wife by socializing with the family and friends. Albert passed away of an intestinal disorder at the age of 54 just two years after marrying Hazel.

===

My grandmother **Isabelle Marie Wilson** (1880 – 1924) followed her older sisters Annie and Georgiana to Pittsfield, Massachusetts. This is a picturesque town in the western part of the state, in a region known as The Berkshires. Like her sisters, she also worked on the production line of a garment factory before she fell in love with a local musician.

Her beloved Abraham Robarge was the son of immigrants from Quebec, Canada and part of a large family himself. Isabelle converted to Roman Catholicism and struggled to learn French to fit in with her soon-to-be extended family. In a romantic act of devotion, Abe Robarge composed a Scott Joplin-style of march-and-two-step dedicated to the love of his life. "The Belle of Berkshire" in 1898 won the Honorable Mention prize from a New York City music publisher's contest.

They had a lovely wedding on November 28, 1901 at the Notre Dame Catholic church in Pittsfield, where Abe Robarge served as the organist. Isabelle's sister Georgiana Wilson served as maid of honor. The *Roanoke Times* proudly announced that a "Roanoke Lady Married" and described the social event in great detail. Isabelle's bridal gown of light blue cotton broadcloth had white silk and ecru trimmings. A bouquet of white roses and smilax flowers crowned her auburn hair, piled up in the soft-styled bun fashionable at the time. The Pittsfield Musicians' Union gave the couple a stylish Morris chair. The Notre Dame Church choir pooled their money to buy a mahogany center table as a wedding present.

In their 20 years of marriage, Isabelle bore six children including my father. Of all the Wilson siblings, my grandmother had the largest family. Abe and Belle Robarge remained in the same home at 36 N. Pearl Street within a stone's throw of the Notre Dame Church for every day of those two decades.

Sadly, she died in 1924 of tuberculosis at the age of 44. Abe Robarge never remarried; no one could ever replace his Belle of the Berkshires.

===

The youngest daughter **Sadie Wilson** (1882 – 1959) followed in her older sister Annie's rebellious footsteps. As soon as she turned 20 years old, Sadie eloped to marry Virginia native Archibald Alexander Brown in September 1902. They surprised everyone (including her widower father) when they hopped an early train out of town. They obtained a marriage license and held their wedding ceremony at a Methodist church in Bristol. They returned to Roanoke on the midnight train and made a home for themselves in town.

Archie Brown worked as a boilermaker for the railroad which meant relocating a few times to pursue better jobs. In 1910, they lived in the town of Cape Charles on a narrow peninsula off the Virginia coast. When Archie registered for the World War I draft, they lived in Norfolk, Virginia. By the time of the 1930 census, they had returned to Roanoke and shared a home with Sadie's brother Albert at 1204 Patterson Avenue SW — another example of the family hospitality.

They raised two daughters, Helen and Edith, and remained in Roanoke well after Archie's retirement. Their marriage lasted over 50 years. Archie died of a sudden heart attack in 1950 at the age of 70. Sadie lived on as a widow until she passed away in 1959.

===

The youngest son, **Walter Scott Wilson** (1889 – 1963), nicknamed "Uncle Bub" was so named because the family's folklore claims a distant relation to the Scottish novelist Sir Walter Scott. Like so many anecdotes in the family, I have so far been unable to find evidence of a connection although the surname Satchell also appears in the novelist's family tree. My father told an anecdote about a steamer trunk full of personal letters from the novelist Sir Walter Scott addressed to an unspecified grandmother, but none of my cousins were aware of this rumor. If such a treasure chest ever existed, it has been lost to time.

Walter moved away from Roanoke, the city of his birth, after his father John Wilson passed away in 1910. He joined his sister (my grandmother Isabelle Robarge) in the New England town of Pittsfield, Massachusetts. In the Pittsfield city directory of 1916, Walter Wilson shared a room in his sister's house—yet another example of the Wilson siblings supporting each other on their travels through life. The following year, at the age of 28, he married Abe Robarge's niece Bertha Boyer.

Walter remained in Pittsfield for the rest of his life working at the Eagle Printing & Binding Company. His wife Bertha Wilson died in 1950 after 30 years of marriage, leaving behind her husband and three daughters. Walter Scott Wilson survived his wife for another decade and lived to the age of 74. He died in Pittsfield, Massachusetts in 1963 as the last of the Wilson siblings.

The Legacy

As the Wilson family continued to struggle with their trauma and grief, so did the city of Roanoke. Many other violent crimes occurred and many other perpetrators were punished. Yet the case of "poor Lizzie Wilson" remained fresh in the minds of Virginians for years to come.

Senator John W. Daniel of Virginia made a speech on the floor of the U.S. Senate on February 23, 1889. As part of a larger argument defending the honor and autonomy of the southern states, he mentioned the Lizzie Wilson murder in graphic detail. "She was murdered in cold blood at her mother's and father's door, her throat cut from ear to ear, her young life spilled upon the ground." Then, he argued that the "two colored men" arrested for the crime had more than one fair trial resulting in a hung jury each time. He bragged about the "self-possession and self-restraint" shown by the people of the community, that the "man who was believed by all people to be the man who committed the offense walked out of jail after three trials and no man laid his hand upon him." He went on to complain, "I am tired of hearing the oft-repeated tale in the United States Senate that all the wrongs which are committed between the races in the Southern States are committed by white men, and that the people of my political faith are the only ones who do them."

However, Senator Davis's rosy portrayal of Southern gentlemen's self-restraint and respect for due process of law, in reality, fell short of the truth. The lingering memory of Lizzie Wilson's brutal murder, and the perceived injustice of her accused killers walking out of jail, fueled the outrage of the white community. Throughout the 1890s, it became a widely accepted viewpoint that lynching was a justifiable response to the presumed epidemic of Black men assaulting white women.

As the civil rights activist Ida B. Wells explained in her speech in January 1900, statistics collected by the *Chicago Tribune* showed that the victims of lynching were accused of all sorts of non-violent offenses including the vague crime of "insulting women." She highlighted an egregious case from 1892 in Louisiana, where a man's blameless fourteen-year-old daughter and sixteen-year-old son were hanged, and their bodies filled with bullets, before their father was also lynched. Lynch mobs shamelessly carried out their grisly business in the broad light of day. Not only was lynching condoned by a community but often they turned into a celebratory carnival. Crowds of women and children often gathered to watch a public spectacle of torture and execution; macabre trophy souvenirs of the scene and photographic postcards were widely popular.

===

The city of Roanoke had its worst moment of madness on a late September day in 1893. Known as the "Riot of 1893" it stands out as a rare instance where the authorities used lethal force in attempting to protect a Black man from a white lynch mob.

The day began with a white woman named Sallie Bishop selling fruit at the city's open-air market. She claimed that a Black man robbed her of a few dollars, threatened her with a razor, and battered her in the head with a brick. Outraged citizens seized upon a man named Thomas Smith at the railway station. Mrs. Bishop — still bleeding from blows to her head — identified him only by the type of floppy hat that he wore. Smith was taken to jail despite his claims of innocence.

Within hours, a large crowd clamoring for revenge approached the jailhouse. The mayor of the city, Henry S. Trout, made an impassioned speech to try and de-escalate the rising outrage. A decade earlier, he had participated in a citizens' meeting and offered a reward for information leading to the capture of Lizzie Wilson's murderer. Back then, it had been enough to print a warning in the newspaper: "We sincerely hope that in the interest of justice, as well as for the good name of the city, our people will keep cool and the wiser control the restless spirits...." Yet on this day, the mayor's eloquent speeches failed to disperse the crowd.

Mayor Trout called up the local militia to clear the streets and defend the prisoner. As darkness fell, more enraged men—including Sallie Bishop's eldest son—swarmed into town from the surrounding farmlands. Thousands of angry men surrounded the jailhouse. Curses and shouting intensified. Tempers flared. Both sides made a stand-off daring each other to make the first move.

Around 8:00 pm, a wild shot rang out. The militia reacted and opened fire. Within minutes, hundreds of rounds were exchanged between the militia's riflemen and the pistol-toting would-be lynchers. The panicked crowd scattered and fled in all directions. Eight men lay dead, including curious onlookers who were in the wrong place at the wrong time. More than 30 others were wounded.

Mayor Trout himself caught a bullet in his foot. He limped to the nearby Hotel Ponce de Leon to take refuge. The mayor ordered the police chief John F. Terry to safeguard the prisoner above all else. Despite his reluctance, Chief Terry obeyed orders; he and a few officers slipped Thomas Smith out the back door to hide in a secluded spot.

Meanwhile, members of the mob turned to ransacking local hardware stores downtown to steal rifles and dynamite. When the mob broke into the jail and found the cells empty, one of the leaders climbed onto a table. He swung a coil of rope and called for volunteers to help him "hang the mayor." Several harrowing hours passed. The mob divided into squads going from house to house searching for both Mayor Trout or the prisoner. They guarded the railway depot to prevent anyone from escaping town.

By the early hours of the morning, Chief Terry made the fateful decision to acquiesce to the lynch mob's demands. He brought Thomas Smith out from his hiding place and threw him to the wolves.

The lynch mob dragged Thomas Smith to the corner of Franklin Road and Mountain Avenue. They hanged him from a hickory tree, riddled his body with bullets, and left him there as a spectacle for the sunrise. When morning came, hundreds of Roanoke's residents turned out to view the ghastly scene.

However, despite the dawn of a new day, the lynch mob was not yet satisfied. They refused to release the mutilated corpse to the city's coroner. Instead, they devised a macabre plan to lay Smith's body on the mayor's dining room table.

Reverend William C. Campbell confronted the howling mob as they proceeded to drag their grisly trophy down the street. The reverend seized hold of the rope by which the corpse was being dragged. He pleaded with the crowd to stop. He managed to dissuade them, at least, from going to the mayor's home. Instead, they dragged the body to the Roanoke River where they built a pyre out of sticks, doused Smith with coal oil, and set him on fire.

Eventually, in the days to follow, order was restored to the city. Newspapers across the country condemned the lawlessness and praised the heroism of the mayor. Reverend Campbell described the sobering mood that followed in the wake of the riot. "It was a terrible lesson to our city. The lesson impressed upon the mind of everyone was that lynching is not the way to punish crime, no matter how aggravating the circumstances may be."

Epilogue

Lizzie Wilson is buried in the Roanoke City Cemetery on Tazewell Avenue in the southeast part of town. The city council donated a burial plot to the grieving family, though it was not the sort of charitable gift they ever would have wished for. Her gravesite was covered with a white marble slab and adorned with the statue of a kneeling lamb.

This cemetery is the oldest and most historically significant final resting place for many respectable citizens of the area since the days when Roanoke was called Big Lick. Sharing this space with the bricklayer's murdered daughter are such locally prominent names as John Trout, his son Henry Trout, Peyton Terry, Reuben Fishburne, and Ferdinand Rorer.

Over the years, wandering milk cows, random acts of vandalism, and general neglect have taken their toll. Many of the tombstones are broken. The wrought iron fences are tainted with rust. On Lizzie Wilson's grave, someone long ago broke the lamb statue and damaged the name carved into her headstone.

In her tragic death, Lizzie Wilson achieved a sad sort of fame that endures to the present day. The annual Halloween Ghost Tour has escorted scores of visitors to various places in and around the city of Roanoke that are said to be haunted. Stories of the supernatural are abundant in Roanoke's antebellum mansions, shuttered theaters, dilapidated hotels, and cemeteries. The lynching tree from which Thomas Smith was hanged in the Riot of 1893 withered and died soon afterward—some said as a judgment of Heaven upon the foul deed committed on that spot. There are tales of a Lady in White who died during the Spanish flu of 1918 and still wanders the City Cemetery in search of her lost children. Of course, the gravesite of poor Lizzie Wilson, the 14-year-old girl who never made it home, is always a featured star on any Ghost Tour.

For my family, her story is more than just a spooky tale whispered by flashlight to curious sightseers walking through the weeds of an old cemetery. Lizzie Wilson was my grandmother's older sister and my father's great-aunt that he never knew. When I look at the fading black-and-white photographs of my father's aunts and uncles, I see a lingering sadness in all of their eyes. They struggled to forget the horror of the past. It has taken me decades of research to follow the breadcrumbs and rediscover the painful episode that affected them all.

Journeying into the past has revealed to me what my ancestors endured, how their dreams for a better life were shattered by one random act of violence, and how they found the strength to persevere.

The End

1883 Map of Roanoke

This is one of the earliest maps of Roanoke showing the city's downtown (lower left-hand corner), the train station and N&W Shops (middle and right), and residential areas (north and northeast)

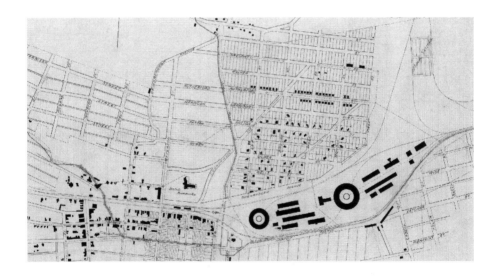

SOURCE: Norfolk & Western Historical Society

Brick Row

The Wilson family lived in this part of southeast Roanoke when they first arrived in town.

SOURCE: John Nolen (1907) Remodeling Roanoke:
Report to the Committee on Civil Improvements

Train Station

The Norfolk & Western Railway passenger station is the hub of downtown Roanoke. The Wilsons came through this depot whenever they travelled in or out of town.

SOURCE: Jacobs, E. B. (1907). Roanoke Virginia

Hotel Roanoke

Lizzie's father John Wilson, a brick mason, participated in the original construction of this landmark building.

She passed nearby while walking home on the night of the murder.

Sheriff Charles Webber

He investigated the Lizzie Wilson murder
and made numerous arrests.

Rev. William C. Campbell

He comforted the Wilson family after Lizzie's murder and helped with arrangements for the funeral and burial.

SOURCE: (1912) History of Roanoke

Henry S. Trout

A prominent citizen who offered a cash reward for information leading to the capture of Lizzie's murderer. He later served as mayor of Roanoke during the Riot of 1893.

SOURCE: (1912) History of Roanoke

Roanoke City Courthouse & Jail

The courthouse, city hall and jail in downtown Roanoke, Virginia at the southwest corner of Campbell Avenue and Second Street. Circa 1887 – 1914. The photograph's original description says that the jail and courthouse were noted for poor housekeeping and some petty graft.

This is the building where the men accused of murdering Lizzie were first confined.

.

Roanoke City Courthouse & Jail

Another view of the courthouse, city hall and jail in downtown Roanoke from a different perspective. Circa 1915.

Roanoke County Courthouse

The original Roanoke County Courthouse (circa 1900) in the nearby town of Salem stood from 1841 to 1909 until a new courthouse was constructed as a replacement.

SOURCE: Salem Historical Society

Roanoke County Courthouse

Interior of the original Roanoke County Courthouse, showing the judge's bench and portraits of local notable persons on the walls. This is the view that the men accused of murdering Lizzie Wilson would have faced.

SOURCE: Salem Historical Society

Lynchburg Courthouse

Courthouse in the town of Lynchburg VA where one of several criminal trials was held for the men accused of murdering Lizzie.

An undated postcard image of the Old Court House built in 1855 on Court Street at Ninth Street, at the top of Monument Terrace. This building was later demolished.

The Judge

Wingfield Griffin, the judge at one of several criminal trials for the men accused of murdering Lizzie Wilson.

The Prosecutor

Mr. Woodrum, the prosecutor at one of the criminal trials for the men accused of murdering Lizzie Wilson.

SOURCE: (1912) History of Roanoke

Defense Attorney

Col. G. W. Hansborough, one of the defense attorneys for the men accused of murdering Lizzie Wilson.

Defense Attorney

J. Allan Watts one of the defense attorneys for the men accused of murdering Lizzie Wilson.

Riot of 1893

Photograph of the courthouse and city hall in downtown Roanoke VA circa 1893 at the time of the riot and lynching of Thomas Smith. Militia men with rifles are in the street.

Ida B. Wells

A prominent African-American journalist and civil rights activist who led an anti-lynching crusade in the United States in the 1890s.

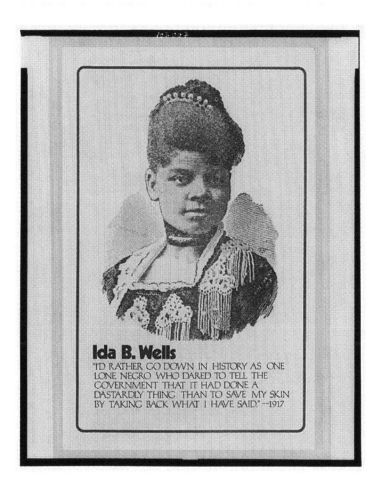

SOURCE: Yanker Poster Collection, Library of Congress Prints and Photographs Division Washington, D.C. 20540 USA

Lizzie Wilson's Birth Record

Original birth registration of Elizabeth Jane Wilson, born on 28 August 1870, in Friern Barnet, Middlesex, England. Her father is listed as John Wilson, a bricklayer. Her mother is listed as Elizabeth Jane Wilson, maiden name Edwards.

Superintendent Registrar's District	*Barnet*							

Registrar's District *Finchley*

18*70* . BIRTHS in the District of *Finchley* in the County of *Middlesex*

No.	When and Where Born.	Name, if any.	Sex.	Name and Surname of Father.	Name and Maiden Surname of Mother.	Rank or Profession of Father.	Signature, Description, and Residence of Informant.	When Registered.	Signature of Registrar.	Baptismal Name if added after Registration of Birth.
496	Twenty eighth August 1870 Amiwell Road Friern Barnet	Elizabeth Jane	Girl	John Wilson	Elizabeth Jane Wilson formerly Edwards	Bricklayer	Elizabeth Jane Wilson Mother Amiwell Road Friern Barnet	Twenty seventh September 1870	James Fox Registrar	

SOURCE: General Register Office, Southport, England U.K. Volume 3A, page 18

1871 U.K. Census

Household of John Wilson, bricklayer, in the town of Friern Barnet, Middlesex, England.

The youngest daughter ("Jane") is Elizabeth Jane Wilson who was 7 months old at the time the census was taken on 2 April 1871.

No. of Schedule	ROAD, STREET, &c., and No. or NAME of HOUSE	HOUSES Inhabited / Uninhabited / Building	NAME and Surname of each Person	RELATION to Head of Family	CON-DITION	AGE of Males / Females	Rank, Profession, or OCCUPATION	WHERE BORN	
69	Cromwell Road	1	John Wilson	Head	mar.		Bricklayer	Warwicksh. Rugby	
			Jane do	Wife	mar.	27		Surrey Godalming	
			Harry do	Son		7		London Hoxton	
			Alice do	Daur		5		Kent Deptford	
			William do	Son		2		Middx Ashley Works	
			Jane do	Daur.		7m		do do	
70			Robert Wardacre	Lodger	mar.		Brickmaker	Cambridgesh. Ely	
			Hannah do	do	mar.	50		do of London Fleet	

1873 Ship's Passenger List

Excerpt of the original ship's passenger arrival record for "Jane Wilson" and her 5 children Harry, Alice, Wm., Eliza, and Anne.

They departed from Liverpool, England on 9 October 1873 and arrived in the port of Quebec, Canada on 20 October 1873 aboard the steamship *Caspian.*

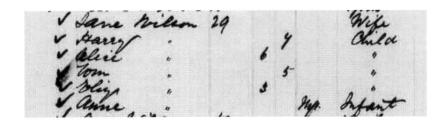

SOURCE: Library and Archives of Canada, "Passenger Lists for the Port of Quebec City and Other Ports, 1865-1922"

The Ship

Representative example of a passenger and cargo steamship, similar in size and design to the S.S. *Caspian* on which the Wilson family crossed the Atlantic Ocean. This is the steamship *Agamemnon*

State Library of Queensland
John Oxley Library

1880 U.S. Census

Excerpt from the federal census of Cleveland, Ohio showing the household of John Wilson, brick mason, his wife Elizabeth and his children: Harry, Alice, William, Elizabeth, Anna, Georgiana, and Albert.

Cleveland Steel Mill

Lizzie's older brother Harry Wilson worked at the Cleveland Rolling Mill in Cleveland, Ohio when he was only 15 years old.

View looking north. - Central Furnaces, 2650 Broadway, east bank of Cuyahoga River, Cleveland, Cuyahoga County, OH

Roanoke Death Register

Excerpt of the original "Register of City of Roanoke Deaths for 1884"

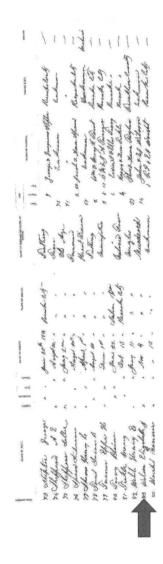

The Grave

Lizzie Wilson's grave in Roanoke's City Cemetery showing the toll that the years have taken, the soil erosion and the broken headstone

1900 U.S. Census

Excerpt from the federal census of Roanoke, Virginia showing the household of John Wilson, brick layer, his wife Elizabeth and three of his children Albert, "Saty" and Walter who are living at home.

Mrs. Wilson passed away 5 months later.

List of the Wilson's Children

Scrap of handwritten notes, circa 1955, created by Myrtle Wilson the daughter of Harry G. Wilson. For years, this was my primary source for the list of 10 children and estimates of the death dates for Myrtle's grandparents John and Elizabeth Jane Wilson.

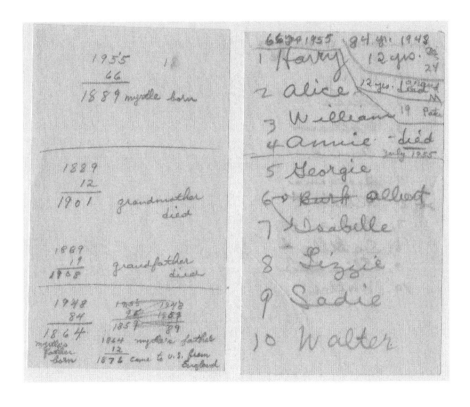

1912 Family Group

This group portrait, dated 1912, was taken on the porch of my grandfather Abe Robarge's home in Pittsfield, Massachusetts:

adults (*left – right*) Abraham Robarge holding his infant son Louis, Walter Scott Wilson, Isabelle Wilson Robarge, Anne Wilson Garland;
children (*left – right*) Arthur, Corinne and Geraldine Robarge, and Charles Garland

1924 Family group

This group portrait was taken on the porch of Abe Robarge's home in Pittsfield, MA, probably for Isabelle's funeral.

(*left to right, back row*) Henry Robarge – the brother of Abraham Robarge, **Harry G. Wilson**, Bertha Boyer Wilson – the wife of Walter Scott Wilson;
(*left to right, middle row*) Arthur or Louis Robarge, **Alice Wilson Dickinson** and **Walter Scott Wilson**;
(*left to right, front row*) my father Woodrow Wilson Robarge, and three unidentified children

Harry G. Wilson

This photograph of Lizzie's eldest brother, circa 1939, is from a newspaper article about the Metropolis Building Association, of which he was president.

Georgina Wilson Lyles

This photograph of Lizzie's younger sister, circa late 1930s, may have been taken by my father's camera.

Albert Wilson's Birth Record

Original registration of Lizzie's younger brother Albert Wilson born in Stratford, Ontario on 03 January 1978. This is my only sample of the father John Wilson's signature.

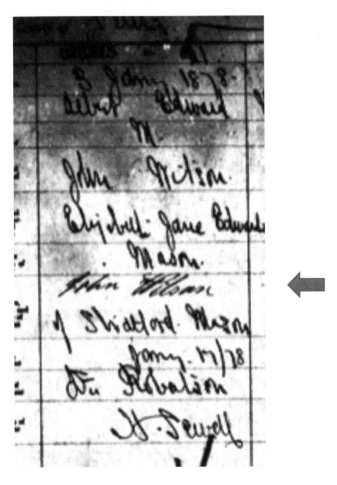

Albert Wilson's Job

Lizzie's younger brother Albert Wilson worked as a coach painter at the Norfolk & Western Shops in Roanoke.

This photograph shows workers painting or stenciling letters onto train cars.

SOURCE: Norfolk & Western Historical Society

Isabelle Marie Wilson

This photograph of Lizzie's younger sister, my grandmother, was taken at the time of her wedding to Abraham Robarge (circa November 1901)

Woodrow Wilson Robarge

This photograph of my father was taken at the time of his graduation from high school.

Bibliography

Miscellaneous references cited in the text are not itemized here due to the sheer volume of materials, including: articles in historical newspapers; official records of birth, marriage, and death; U.S. and U.K. census returns; city directories, online encyclopedias, etc.

Websites

- *Ancestry.* https://www.ancestry.com
- *Family Search.* https://www.familysearch.org
- *Library of Congress, Digitized Historical Newspapers.* https://chroniclingamerica.loc.gov
- *Library of Congress, Prints & Photographs Online Catalog,* http://www.loc.gov/pictures
- *Find A Grave (the world's largest gravesite collection)* https://www.findagrave.com
- *Free BMD (U.K. birth-marriage-death indexes)* https://www.freebmd.org.uk
- *Historical Society of Western Virginia.* https://roanokehistory.org
- *Lynchburg Museum at the Old Court House* https://www.lynchburgphotos.org
- *Salem Museum & Historical Society* https://salemmuseum.org
- *The City of Roanoke (links to public libraries)* https://www.roanokeva.gov
- *Virginia Memory. The Library of Virginia.* https://www.virginiamemory.com

Published Books and Articles

Barnes, R. P. (1968). A history of Roanoke. Radford, Va.: Commonwealth Press.

Biesenbach, Betsy. "Driving tour of Roanoke history." Special to The Roanoke Times. Oct 5, 2014

BlackPast, B. (2010, July 13). (1900) Ida B. Wells, "Lynch Law in America". BlackPast.org. https://www.blackpast.org/african-american-history/1900-ida-b-wells-lynch-law-america/

Bruce, T. (1891). Southwest Virginia and Shenandoah Valley: An Inquiry Into the Causes of the Rapid Growth and Wonderful Development of Southwest Virginia and Shenandoah Valley, with a History of the Norfolk and Western and Shenandoah Valley Railroads .... United States: Hill Publishing Company.

Campbell, Rev. W.C. "Older Inhabitant Recalls Some of the Tragedies of the City." *The World News*. Roanoke, VA. March 29, 1927. William Creighton Campbell Papers. Historical Society of Western Virginia.

Chittum, Matt. "When segregation ruled the streets: A largely forgotten chapter of Roanoke's racial history emerges from the work of an ambitious summer intern.". *The Roanoke Times*. August 14, 2005.

Daniel, J. W. (1889). State Rights ...: Speech of Hon. John W. Daniel, of Virginia, in the Senate of United States, Saturday, February 23, 1889. United States: (n.p.).

Dotson, R. (2008). Roanoke, Virginia, 1882-1912: Magic City of the New South. United States: University of Tennessee Press.

Garner, Glenna Garnand, Roanoke City VA Archives Cemeteries....City Cemetery. Tazewell Ave. SE, Roanoke, VA. USGenWeb Archives. June 6, 2009

Jack, George S., Jacobs, E. B. (1912). History of Roanoke County. United States: Stone Printing & Mfg. Co.

Jacobs, E. B. (1907). Roanoke Virginia: Its Location, Climate and Water Supply; Its Manufacturing, Commercial and Educational Advantages and General Desirability as a Place of Residence. United States: Stone Printing & Mfg. Co.

Kittredge, Kevin. "Pillars of the Past", *The Roanoke Times*, October 30, 2010

Long, John D. (2019) Murder in Roanoke County: Race and Justice in the 1891 Susan Watkins Case. The History Press.

Nolen, John (1907) Remodeling Roanoke: Report to the Committee on Civil Improvements, by John Nolen, Landscape Architect, Cambridge, Massachusetts. Roanoke, VA: Stone Printing & Mfg. Co.

About the Author

Denise B. Tanaka has a lifelong passion for writing stories of magical beings and faraway worlds but is sometimes sidetracked by nonfiction projects. A graduate of Sonoma State University, she works as a senior paralegal in immigration law. She has dabbled in genealogy for more than 30 years and is very grateful for the internet.

Made in the USA
Columbia, SC
31 October 2022

70290423R00113